LOST CAPITALS *of* ALABAMA

HERBERT JAMES LEWIS

THE History PRESS

Published by The History Press
Charleston, SC 29403
www.historypress.net

First published 2014

Manufactured in the United States

ISBN 978.1.62619.442.7

Library of Congress CIP data applied for.

Notice: The information in this book is true and complete to the best of our knowledge. It is offered without guarantee on the part of the author or The History Press. The author and The History Press disclaim all liability in connection with the use of this book.

This book is dedicated
to my daughter and granddaughter—

Emily Lewis Rich and Elizabeth Roper Rich

Contents

Preface

I developed a passion for early Alabama history as a child when my father took me around the state on weekend excursions to many of Alabama's historical sites. Among those was an excursion to Lowndes County, where we searched for the point where William Weatherford, later dubbed "Red Eagle" by poet A.B. Meek, purportedly jumped into the Alabama River to escape American soldiers at the Battle of the Holy Ground. Other weekend trips included visits to Horseshoe Bend National Park; Moundville; the ruins of old Cahaba, which is a subject of this book; and antebellum homes in the Black Belt. I fondly remember studying Alabama history in the fourth grade, with our textbook entitled *Know Alabama*, and in the ninth grade, studying Summersell's *Alabama.* Also, at some point during my teenage years, my father introduced me to Alabama's first history, A.J. Picket's *History of Alabama and Incidentally of Georgia and Mississippi from the Earliest Period*, which was written in 1851.

Although a lawyer by profession, I majored in history in undergraduate school, which further contributed to my passion for the history of early Alabama. After thirty-one years of practicing law, mostly as an assistant United States attorney in Birmingham, Alabama, I retired in January 2006 and began to devote my time to researching and writing about early Alabama history. In April 2006, the *Alabama Review* published my article about my third great-grandfather Henry Wilbourne Stevens, who migrated to Alabama in 1814 from Connecticut, where he had attended the Litchfield Law School and had been admitted to the bar of that state.

Stevens's practice of law in the new territory would have to wait, as his arrival in Mobile coincided with the need for more men to serve in the Mississippi territorial militia during the closing months of the War of 1812. Accordingly, Stevens served in the militia for just three months before he was discharged from the service in March 1815. A few months later, he was commissioned by the territorial governor to practice law in the Mississippi Territory. He then practiced law for a short while near Natchez before succumbing to Alabama fever and becoming Montgomery County's first justice of the peace and register of its orphans' court in 1816. In September 1818, Stevens was appointed by territorial governor William Wyatt Bibb to serve as a justice of the quorum in Cahawba County.

After publication of the Stevens article, I was determined to conduct further research with regard to antebellum Alabama. Luckily, I was soon contacted by representatives of the Alabama Humanities Foundation and the *Encyclopedia of Alabama* to become a freelance writer and editor for the encyclopedia. In that capacity, I contributed forty-seven entries, almost half of which pertain to early Alabama history. The research for those entries inspired in me the idea of writing a book to tell the story of Alabama from frontier times until the eve of the Civil War. That book, entitled *Clearing the Thickets: A History of Antebellum Alabama*, was published in March 2013 by Quid Pro Books in New Orleans, Louisiana. It focuses on the political, constitutional and military developments of Alabama's antebellum period, as well as the social and economic transformations that were occurring during this time frame and how they were interrupted and stunted by the tragedy of secession and war. This was the first general history written about Alabama's antebellum period in almost twenty years.

A few months after the publication of *Clearing the Thickets*, I was contacted by The History Press to gauge my interest in writing a book pertaining to the lost capitals of Alabama. I was delighted to do so, not only because of my keen interest in the history of antebellum Alabama, but also because it has been sixty-seven years since any significant book has been written about Alabama's previous capitals. In 1947, William H. Brantley Jr. wrote a book entitled *Three Capitals: A Book About the First Three Capitals of Alabama: St. Stephens, Huntsville, and Cahawba, 1818–1826*. For some reason, Brantley chose not to examine Tuscaloosa in his work. While this book freshly reexamines Alabama's first three capitals and their fates, it will also examine the significant role that Tuscaloosa played for twenty years as the state's last capital before Montgomery became the permanent capital in 1846. Two of the lost capitals, St. Stephens and Cahaba, eventually became virtual ghost towns after losing their status of capital. The other two capitals, Huntsville and Tuscaloosa, survived and excelled. They are both, of course, vibrant cities today. All of them, however, are rich with history and were instrumental in Alabama's formative period as a state. This book will examine each in detail, along with their leaders; significant events; their economic, social and cultural developments; and their fates after the seat of government left them.

Acknowledgements

There are many people deserving of acknowledgement with respect to the publication of this book. First and foremost are Dr. Jeff Jakeman and Steve Murray. Dr. Jakeman, of Auburn University, was editor of the *Alabama Review* when I sought advice about how to have my article relating to Henry Wilbourne Stevens considered for publication for the *Review*. His encouragement to take a shot at it put me on the road to my first publication concerning early Alabama history. Steve Murray, now director of the Alabama Department of Archives and History, was managing editor of the *Alabama Review* when I submitted my article to the *Review*. I went through a very detailed editing process with Steve, who showed great patience with a novice writer such as myself. Steve later sought me out to contribute a few entries for the new *Encyclopedia of Alabama* (*EOA*), which led me to contract as a freelance writer and editor for the *EOA* through the Alabama Humanities Foundation.

My experience working with the *EOA* proved to be invaluable to me, for which I am indebted to the entire *EOA* staff starting with Dr. Wayne Flynt, editor in chief. In addition to Jeff Jakeman and Steve Murray, I also need to acknowledge James P. Kaetz, managing editor; Claire Wilson, senior content editor; Christopher Maloney, content editor; Laura Newland Hill, communications director; Benjamin Berntson, *EOA*'s former production editor; and Donna Siebenthaler, formerly a graduate research assistant for *EOA*.

Others to whom I owe a debt of gratitude with regard to my writing projects include Dr. Leah Rawls Atkins, former director of the Auburn

University Center for the Arts and Humanities; Dr. Paul Pruitt Jr., Collection Development & Special Collections Librarian, Bounds Law Library, University of Alabama School of Law; James L. Noles Jr., lawyer, author and former chairman of the board of directors of the Alabama Humanities Foundation; Martin Everse, former director of Tannehill Historical State Park and Brierfield Ironworks Historical State Park; Dr. James S. Day, assistant vice-president of academic affairs and associate professor of history at the University of Montevallo; Robert Stewart, former executive director of the Alabama Humanities Foundation; Garland Cook Smith, Wilcox County Historical Society; Bobby Joe Seales, president of the Shelby County Historical County; Elizabeth C. Wells, former coordinator of the Special Collections Department, Samford University Library, Birmingham, Alabama; the research staff at the Alabama Department of Archives and History (ADAH), Montgomery, Alabama; the staff of the North Shelby County Library; and the staff of the Linn-Henley Library, Birmingham, Alabama. A special recognition is due to Meredith McDonough of the ADAH and Susanna Leberman with the special collections section of the Huntsville–Madison County Public Library.

Finally, I must thank my wife, Becky Lewis; my daughter, Emily L. Rich; and my son-in-law, Joey Rich, who have all supported my various projects. I also must mention my granddaughter, Elizabeth Roper Rich; I hope this book will help her to appreciate Alabama history as she grows older.

Introduction

Before Montgomery became Alabama's capital in 1846, the state had seen four capitals come and go—St. Stephens, Huntsville, Cahaba and Tuscaloosa. All of these capitals were subjected to the politics of the times and lost their status as seats of government. It was not unusual for states in their formative years to have several different capitals before settling on a permanent capital. For example, the capital of Georgia moved back and forth several times between Savannah and Augusta and also met in Louisville, Milledgeville and Macon before settling on Atlanta in 1868. Mississippi serves as another example of a state having multiple capitals, with Natchez, Washington and Columbia serving in that capacity until the capital was finally located in Jackson in 1832. In his introduction to the reprint of William H. Brantley Jr.'s 1947 book written about Alabama's first three capitals, historian Malcolm C. McMillan referred to Alabama's early capitals as "frontier capitals on wheels."

Alabama's eventual need for a capital was set in motion when it became part of the Mississippi Territory created by Congress in 1798. As the population of the territory increased, a debate began over whether the territory would seek admission to the Union as one state or as two states. At first, the more numerous residents of the western portion of the territory opposed the creation of two states. But because of the perceived need to keep pace with the admission of non-slave states, southern senators opposed an 1812 bill that would have admitted the entire Mississippi Territory as one state. Ironically, the eastern section residents in the Tombigbee and Tensaw districts would later favor admission of the territory as one state because of the increase in their population after the seizure of Mobile from Spain in 1813 and the close of the Creek War of 1813–14. Meanwhile, the western residents began to favor admission as two states in order to protect their population base in the Natchez area along the Mississippi River. This position finally prevailed due to the persistent congressional sentiment for a balance of power between the slave and non-slave states. Accordingly, the western section of the territory was admitted to the Union as the state of Mississippi in March 1817, and the eastern section then became the Alabama Territory.

The Alabama section of the old Mississippi Territory was now on its own and was in need of a capital. The honor of becoming the first capital in Alabama history was afforded to St. Stephens, a former Spanish fort and trading post located approximately sixty-seven miles north of Mobile in present-day Washington County. It had the distinction of being the first and only capital of the Alabama Territory, serving in that capacity between 1817 until 1819. Because of its short reign as Alabama's first seat of government, no permanent capitol building was constructed there. The town grew rapidly while it served as capital but shrank in prominence after the capital moved temporarily to Huntsville in 1819 until such time as the town of Cahaba could be laid out. By 1833, St. Stephens was just a small village and was in total ruins by the eve of the Civil War.

The temporary removal of the capital to Huntsville was the result of political maneuvering between south and north Alabama. In essence, Alabama's first governor, William Wyatt Bibb, used his connections in Washington to secure passage of a bill that granted a free section of land for use as the state's seat of government and gave the governor the prerogative to select the site. Bibb chose a site at the confluence of the Alabama and Cahaba Rivers then referred to as "Cahawba" (referred to as "Cahaba" since the 1850s). While Tuscaloosa was the choice of a commission that had been chosen by the legislature to recommend the capital's location, Bibb attached a rider to an apportionment bill favorable to north Alabama that provided for Cahaba to become the state's capital. To further placate northern representatives, Huntsville was selected as the temporary capital until Cahaba was made ready to serve as the state's permanent capital. Although Huntsville's reign as capital was even shorter than that of St. Stephens, nevertheless, while in Huntsville, a constitution was adopted, and the first session of the state's General Assembly was held to begin passing legislation to fill in the framework of government provided for by the constitution. After the capital moved to Cahaba, Huntsville continued to thrive as an important city. Today, it is renowned for its role in the nation's modern space program and serves as one of the New South's leading technology centers.

With the completion of the first session of the state's General Assembly at Huntsville, all of the state's officeholders began the long trek to the new capital at Cahaba. Although Governor Bibb was successful in out-maneuvering the proponents for Tuscaloosa as the state capital, steps were taken in the Constitutional Convention to give the Tuscaloosa supporters another shot at obtaining the capital. In this regard, they passed a constitutional provision designating Cahaba as the capital until 1825, at which time the General Assembly was given the option to relocate the capital without the governor's concurrence. If this option were not exercised, Cahaba would remain as the capital. Until that time, Cahaba reigned supreme in the middle of the wilderness of the Alabama frontier and became the focus of political, as well as cultural, life in Alabama. Unfortunately, as every effort was being made to complete construction of the capitol in Cahaba, Governor Bibb, already in poor health, died on August 20, 1820, as a result of injuries sustained when he fell from his horse. Cahaba had lost its most ardent supporter. Nevertheless, the new city in the wilderness grew rapidly with completion of the capitol building and the arrival of politicians, businessmen, lawyers and physicians. The population continued to grow until politics intervened, resulting in Cahaba losing its status as capital in 1825. Before state government left, however, Cahaba had the distinction of playing host to the Marquis de Lafayette, the last surviving general of the American Revolution, who was on a grand tour of the United States in honor of the nation's fiftieth anniversary. Lafayette's tour was perhaps the most exciting event in Cahaba's brief history.

As the excitement of Lafayette's visit diminished in Cahaba, the 1825 session of the General Assembly met to decide Cahaba's fate as the state's capital. This time, the Tuscaloosa supporters, aided by flooding and health concerns, prevailed in passing a bill to have the capital moved to Tuscaloosa, effective on February 1, 1826. Cahaba faltered for a while thereafter but boomed again in the 1840s and '50s with the influx of wealthy cotton planters taking advantage of the rich Black Belt soil and the increase in river traffic. The beginning of the Civil War, however, put a damper on Cahaba's boom. With the loss of its railroad terminus and the loss of its status as county seat of Dallas County, Cahaba's population began to decrease drastically. By 1870, there were only about three hundred people—mostly freed slaves—remaining in Cahaba. By the turn of the century, Cahaba was virtually a ghost town.

Alabama's government assembled for the first time in Tuscaloosa on November 20, 1826. The state leaders in the first three capitals had dealt primarily with organizing state government. While the capital was in Tuscaloosa for the next twenty years, the state's leaders had to deal with broader national issues such as tariffs, internal improvements, slavery, Indian policy and states' rights. They would also be faced with difficulties presented by the Panic of 1837 and the Creek War of 1836. Only four governors served while the capital was in St. Stephens, Huntsville and Cahaba. While the capital was in Tuscaloosa, however, a total of nine governors served. In addition to being the seat of government, Tuscaloosa, largely because of the presence of the University of Alabama, was also the state's center for education and cultural achievements.

On January 24, 1845, the state legislature passed a joint resolution proposing an amendment to Alabama's constitution to once again make it possible to move the capital. That amendment was ultimately adopted, and several cities sought to take the capital away from Tuscaloosa. Because the population of the state was shifting to the southeast as a result of Creek lands opening up in the 1830s, and because political power was also shifting from the northern part of the state southward to the Black Belt, Montgomery was selected by the legislature to become Alabama's fifth and final capital. Tuscaloosa soon felt the harsh effects of the removal of the capital to Montgomery in terms of a significant loss in population, the plummeting of real estate values and a significant downturn in business. Tuscaloosa commenced a recovery after the Civil War with the reopening of the University of Alabama and the continued presence of the State Hospital for the Insane (later renamed Bryce Hospital). Like Huntsville, Tuscaloosa is today one of Alabama's premier cities, serving as the commercial hub of west-central Alabama, and is home to such large manufacturing firms as Mercedes-Benz, Michelin and JVC.

Alabama's exciting early history evolved for twenty-eight years along the paths that led to the location of its capitals at St. Stephens, Huntsville, Cahaba and Tuscaloosa. During this formative period, the state was molded by the actions of those who held office in these four capitals. This book examines these lost capitals, their leaders, the important events occurring in each, the cultural and social developments in each and the fates of each after losing its status as the state's capital.

CHAPTER 1

ST. STEPHENS

CAPITAL OF ALABAMA TERRITORY

FORMATIVE PERIOD (1736–1816)

Alabama's government originated in the old town of St. Stephens, high atop a limestone bluff overlooking the Tombigbee River, approximately sixty-seven miles north of Mobile in what is now Washington County. This location, referred to as "Hobuckintopa Bluff" by indigenous Choctaw Indians, contained rocky shoals that prevented further river traffic northward. The area had been under the control of the French, English and Spanish until the United States assumed control in 1799. The town of St. Stephens was chartered by the Mississippi Territory in 1811.[1]

The French were the first to rule the area that included St. Stephens, but in 1736, they chose to go beyond the rapids at Hobuckintopa Bluff upriver to construct Fort Tombeckbe, a major fort on the Tombigbee River near present-day Epes in Sumter County, as protection against British traders and local Indians. Hobuckintopa Bluff was nevertheless used as an outpost of sorts from which the French could transfer cargo from their oceangoing vessels onto barges above the shoals to provision Fort Tombeckbe. The Treaty of Paris of 1763, which ended the French and Indian War, passed control of the region to the British. In 1772, surveyor and naturalist Bernard Romans was sent by the British to evaluate the Tombigbee region. Romans recognized the potential for the Hobuckintopa site, stating in his journal, "Sloops and schooners may come up to this rapid: therefore, I judge some considerable settlement will take place." Despite this evaluation, the British did not occupy this site during the seventeen years of its rule of the region.[2]

At the conclusion of the American Revolution, Great Britain agreed to relinquish East and West Florida to Spain. This cession to Spain, however, did not provide a clearly defined northern boundary for the Floridas, resulting in disputed boundary lines that would not be resolved for a little over a decade. While Spanish and American diplomats jockeyed to establish an agreeable boundary, Spanish authorities saw the need to establish a defensive system to protect Spain's colonies in Louisiana and West Florida. In 1789, the Spanish governor in Mobile ordered the construction of the first fortification to be situated atop Hobuckintopa Bluff. This strategic fortification was named Fort Esteban, presumably in honor of Governor Esteban Rodríguez Miró in Mobile. In addition to a blockhouse, the fort was given a sense of stability by the construction of an outer system of protective earthworks, a church and quarters for the fort's commandant. In furtherance of its defensive scheme, in 1794, Spain sent soldiers farther north up the Tombigbee River to take over the old site of Fort Tombeckbe, which the British had renamed Fort York when it was under their control. The fort was in turn given the name Fort Confederation by the Spanish, in recognition of their alliance with local Native American tribes, who served as a buffer against American intrusion.[3]

Spanish control of the future site of Alabama's first capital slipped away with the signing of the Treaty of San Larenzo on October 27, 1795. With this treaty, Spain ceded all of its claims to territory north of the thirty-first parallel. When Spanish officials in the Gulf region learned of the treaty, they immediately complained that Spanish diplomats had given up too much real estate. Although Fort Confederation was evacuated in March 1797, Spanish minister Manuel de Godoy, apparently having listened to the complaints, ordered that further evacuations of posts above the thirty-first parallel be delayed. While further evacuations were delayed for another year, when a survey completed by Andrew Ellicott in 1799 established that Fort San Esteban was located just north of the thirty-first parallel and within American territory, Spain finally decided to abandon its fortification atop Hobuckintopa Bluff. On May 5, 1799, Fort San Esteban's commandant, Antonio Palaas, struck the Spanish colors for the last time and led his troops out. An awaiting contingent of Americans under the command of Lieutenant John McClary then paraded in and raised the flag of the United States over this site for the first time. The fort was now located within the Mississippi Territory, and its name was changed to Fort St. Stephens. Mobile, which was clearly below the thirty-first parallel, remained under Spanish control until it was annexed by the United States in 1813.[4]

With the acquisition of Fort St. Stephens, the way was opened for American colonization of the lower Tombigbee region as settlers came streaming into the area from Georgia along the Federal Road through Creek country, from Virginia and the Carolinas down the Tennessee River and even from the west down the Tombigbee River. In 1803, the federal government sent Indian agent Joseph Chambers to Fort St. Stephens to establish a "factory" known as the Choctaw Trading House. In August 1803, Chambers reported to territorial governor William C.C. Claiborne, "Those Indians who have been to the house to trade, appear to be well satisfied, and they generally conduct themselves in an orderly peaceable and friendly manner towards the white Inhabitants." When Chambers resigned in 1806, George Strothers Gaines replaced him and gained the confidence of the local Choctaws and the settlers along the lower Tombigbee and Tensaw Rivers. Traders, or factors, such as Chambers and Gaines were sent for the purpose of providing superior merchandise to the local Indians at reasonable prices, as well as to encourage their customers to embrace American culture. Trading was vigorous at St. Stephens's Choctaw House because of Gaines's popularity among the Choctaws, as well as because of his sagacity to rely on trading routes that avoided the punitive duties that Spain levied on goods coming through Mobile. The factory store was located in the old Spanish blockhouse constructed in 1789. Gaines's residence was in the home of the former Spanish commandant. When the factory store became "leaky and untenable" in the early part of 1812, Gaines moved the trading house and the land office to a new brick building that he had erected in 1811. Gaines believed that this building was perhaps the first brick building constructed on Alabama soil.[5]

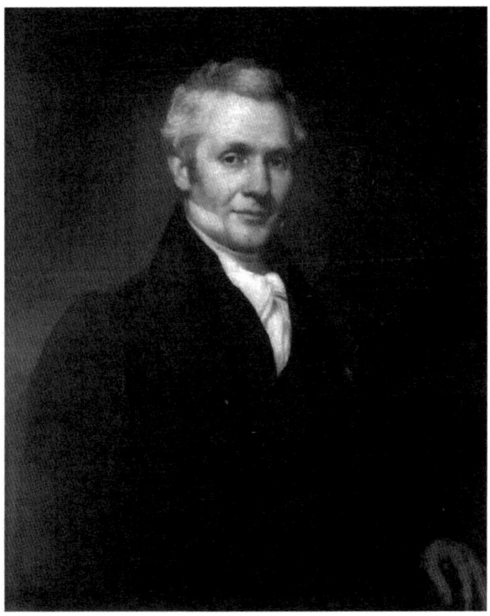

George Strothers Gaines (1784–1873), an Indian agent located in St. Stephens (1804–1815). *Courtesy Alabama Department of Archives and History.*

In 1803, President Thomas Jefferson appointed Ephraim Kirby of Connecticut and Robert Carter Nicholas of Kentucky as land commissioners of the United States in Washington County. They were appointed pursuant to the Congressional Act of March 3, 1803, passed for the purpose of "regulating the grants of land, and providing for the disposal of the lands of the United States, south of the state of Tennessee." Although they first reported for duty at Fort Stoddert a little over thirty miles north of Fort St. Stephens, Kirby wrote to President Jefferson on February 5, 1804, "Fort St. Stephens is more in the center of population, and will be a more convenient place for the permanent establishment of the Register's Office." As a result, the permanent land office was opened in Fort St. Stephens and housed in the old Spanish blockhouse along with the Choctaw Trading House. Joseph Chambers was chosen to be the register of the land office.[6]

The board of land commissioners, led by Ephraim Kirby, worked six days a week between March and July 1804 in order to provide clear title of the lands to area settlers where appropriate. Kirby was soon to take on other duties, however, when he accepted an appointment as the first federal judge to sit in the Alabama portion of the Mississippi Territory at Fort Stoddert. Despite President Jefferson's personal appeal to him, Kirby had been reluctant to accept this appointment, confiding in an earlier letter to a friend that, "should I continue here any great length of time, cut off from all intercourse with the intelligent part of my species I shall forget the relation in which I stand to them," and he wished "for the termination of [his] official duties in this wild region." Kirby again resisted his urge to leave when President Jefferson asked him—apart from his official duties as land commissioner and federal judge—to provide the government with intelligence about the area's physical features, the characteristics of its settlers and the strength of nearby Spanish settlements, including Mobile and Pensacola. His report to the president concerning the area's settlers painted a very bleak picture of the local populace. In this report, he stated that "the present inhabitants (with few exceptions) are illiterate, wild and savage, of depraved morals, unworthy of public confidence and private esteem; litigious, disunited, and knowing each other, universally distrustful of each other." Local officials fared no better; Kirby described them as being "without dignity, respect, probity, influence or authority," leaving local justice in an "imbecile and corrupt" state.[7]

In August 1804, Kirby took ill with a "billous fever" after traveling up the Tombigbee River to Fort St. Stephens during a period of heavy rains. By September, he was somewhat better and contemplated going home to Connecticut to further improve his health. Unfortunately, he had a relapse and died in his quarters at Fort Stoddert on October 20, 1804, and was buried with military honors in the fort's cemetery. Although he had been in the Tombigbee settlements for only nine months, he had brought stability to the area by the establishment of the land office at Fort St. Stephens and by stalling, at least for a while, filibustering activities aimed at Spanish Mobile. Kirby never held court during his brief tenure as territorial judge due to the juggling of his other responsibilities as land commissioner and emissary to President Jefferson, as well as the time he spent investigating the filibustering activities against Spain.[8]

Kirby was succeeded by Harry Toulmin, then serving as Kentucky's secretary of state. Judge Toulmin, a dissenting minister from England who sought refuge in America, soon gained favor with Thomas Jefferson and James Monroe, who gave him letters of introduction. In 1794, he became the president of the Transylvania Seminary in Lexington, Kentucky. After getting crossways with school trustees who were anti-Jeffersonian Federalists as well as conservative Presbyterians, he was appointed as Kentucky's secretary of state. In that position, he undertook a compilation of Kentucky's laws and was a signatory to the Kentucky Resolutions protesting the Alien and Sedition Acts. His certification of the Kentucky Resolutions put him in the further good graces of Thomas Jefferson, so much so that he was appointed by President Jefferson as judge of the Mississippi Territory in 1804 to succeed Ephraim Kirby. When Toulmin arrived in the territory, he moved the county seat of Washington County from McIntosh Bluff to Wakefield, where he presided for many years as the only federal official in the area. By necessity, he wore many hats and, in addition to his judicial duties, served as postmaster, ran a mail route from Fort Stoddert to Natchez, officiated at marriages and funerals and practiced medicine. He was in essence the czar of the Tombigbee settlements, including St. Stephens. During his tenure, he sought to restrain filibusterers in their quest for Spanish Mobile; he was prominently involved in the arrest of former vice president Aaron Burr, who was accused of treasonous activities involving, in part, the possible overthrow of the western states and an attack on Spanish possessions; and he had to keep the rowdy backwoodsmen of his district in check so that order would prevail and the area would be ready for statehood.[9]

In response to the number of settlers arriving in St. Stephens and the surrounding area, the United States postmaster general established a post office at Fort St. Stephens in 1805. As the area near Fort St. Stephens began to attract a commercial class in addition to its original frontiersmen, the citizens in the vicinity petitioned the Mississippi Territorial Assembly to provide

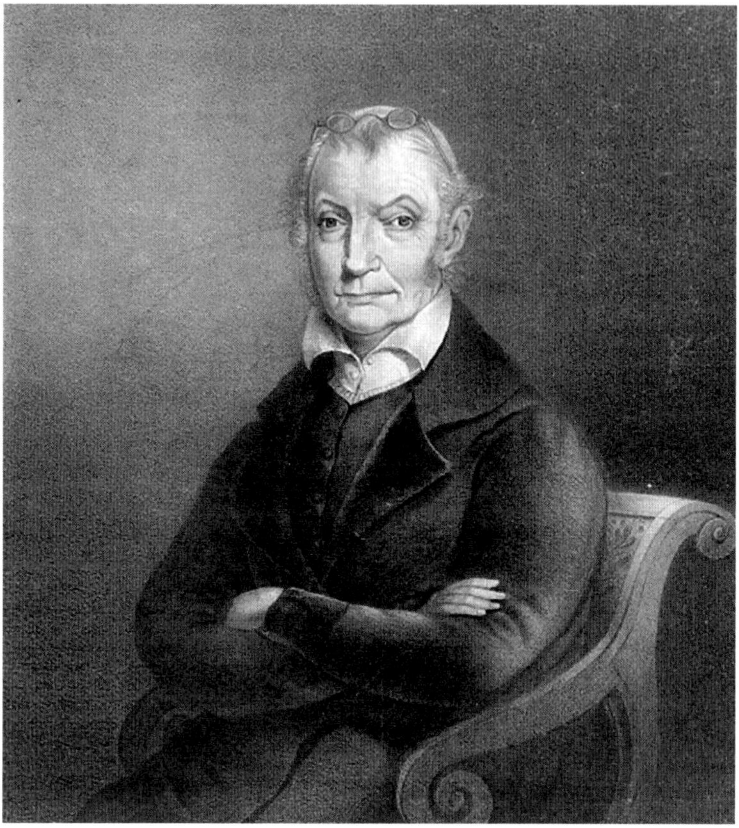

Former vice president Aaron Burr (1756–1836), arrested near St. Stephens on February 19, 1807, was charged with treasonous activities. *Library of Congress.*

them with an organized town in which to live and conduct business on an eighty-acre tract of land near Fort St. Stephens bounded by the Tombigbee River and the lands of John Chastang, Peter Malone and Edwin Lewis. The assembly ultimately responded favorably by incorporating the town of St. Stephens, but there is some confusion about when this actually occurred. On January 8, 1807, the assembly chartered a town to be laid out on the lands of Edwin Lewis[10] on the Tombigbee River near Fort St. Stephens. Many have reported that this act pertained to the town of St. Stephens, but historian Peter Hamilton asserted that this act in fact pertained to the town of Franklin, which was laid out above the fort on the lands of Edwin Lewis. Hamilton appears to be correct since the 1807 act did not give a name to the town but provided that it was to be laid out on the property of Edwin

Lewis. Furthermore, an act passed on December 18, 1811, as amended in 1815, was clearly for the purpose of establishing and incorporating the town of St. Stephens.[11]

On December 18, 1815, Judge Toulmin wrote to William Lattimore, the Mississippi Territory's representative in the U.S. Congress, complaining of the need for additional judges in Washington County and for a better organization of the court system throughout the entire territory. He emphasized that the territorial district for which he was responsible was 340 miles long and 330 miles wide, covering seven present-day counties, mostly in present-day Alabama. He had to cover all of these counties twice a year, which burdened him both physically and in terms of his pocketbook. He therefore urged the appointment of at least two more judges to provide better coverage of the district. In this same letter, he indicated that there was no question that the Supreme Court should sit in St. Stephens twice a year. Acknowledging that only St. Stephens and Mobile had the "appearance of a town," he nevertheless favored St. Stephens as the "most convenient to the thickest population." Furthermore, he indicated that Mobile "was a very small place, and has nothing that can be called a settlement within forty miles of it—and is besides almost at the extreme of the district—so that jurors will have to travel a great distance—if court were held there."[12]

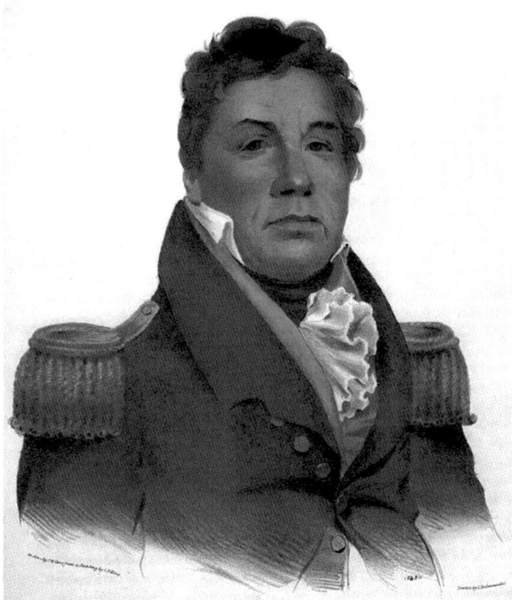

Pushmataha, the Choctaw chieftain who provided support to General Andrew Jackson's forces during the Creek War after he and his warriors assembled at St. Stephens. *Wikimedia Commons.*

While St. Stephens was in its formative stages, the settlers of the lower Tombigbee area began to feel the heightening tension between themselves and the Creek Indian Nation. As early as July 1810, George Strothers Gaines wrote from the Choctaw Trading House to Mingo Poosmataha (Pushmataha), a chief of the Choctaw Nation, complaining that "Creek Indians have threatened our settlements on the Tombigbee with destruction." He further noted that "[w]e don't doubt the friendship of your nation & [are] fearful that some unpleasant mistakes may take place for many may not be able to distinguish a Muscogee from a Choctaw." He therefore requested that Pushmataha order his people to leave the American settlements for a few weeks and to travel on only the main road if they must conduct business in the area. Leading up to the Fort Mims massacre, settlers in the area began "forting up" when hostile Indians were reported in the area. Those seeking refuge included many citizens of Clarke County who fled to St. Stephens and constructed a stockade on a knoll within the town, which was named Fort Republic. On October 21, 1813, after the massacre at Fort Mims, Indian agent John McKee reported to John Coffee, an aide to General Andrew Jackson, that the chiefs and warriors in the Tombigbee area favored war against the Creek Nation. He further indicated that he would soon take fifty warriors to Fort St. Stephens to purchase ammunition if available. Later, in March 1814, McKee wrote to the commanding officer at St. Stephens that he was coming there with five hundred Choctaw and Chickasaw warriors to join the Third Regiment, U.S. Infantry Regulars, commanded by Colonel Gilbert C. Russell. Some of these warriors then accompanied Russell's regiment northward, where they helped defeat the Creeks at the Battle of the Holy Ground. Two years after the end of the Creek War, on October 24, 1816, the Treaty of St. Stephens was entered into between the United States and the Choctaw Nation, whereby ten thousand acres of Choctaw land east of the Tombigbee River was ceded to the United States in exchange for $6,000 annually for a period of twenty years and for the immediate delivery of $10,000 worth of merchandise.[13]

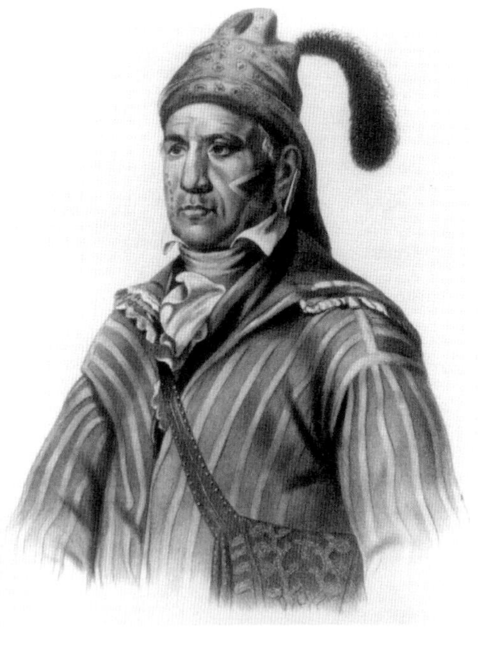

The Creek War of 1813–14 temporarily slowed the growth of St. Stephens. Depicted here is Creek chief Menawa. *Wikimedia Commons.*

On Christmas Day 1804, an itinerant evangelist preacher by the name of Lorenzo Dow arrived in St. Stephens and recorded in his journal that there was only one family residing there but predicted that "it will be a place of fame in time." British surveyor and naturalist Bernard Romans had similarly predicted "a considerable settlement" in 1772. Although these prophecies would eventually be borne out, the growth of St. Stephens would be slow until after the Creek War. According to a letter sent to General Andrew Jackson from A.P. Hayne, the fledgling town had only three houses in 1811, the year of its incorporation, and only nine houses, "and not a good one," by 1815. Just a year later, however, Hayne reported to General Jackson that St. Stephens had approximately forty houses and a business capital of close to $300,000. He further reported that many new houses were being constructed and that lots that could command only $150 in 1815 were going for $600 in 1816. In recognition of its signs of growth, St. Stephens was made the county seat of Washington County by commissioners appointed by an act of the Mississippi Territorial Assembly "to fix the permanent Seat of Justice and to levy a tax to build a courthouse and jail in Washington County."[14]

As the town began to grow, on December 17, 1811, the Mississippi Territorial Assembly authorized the establishment of Alabama's first educational institution to be called the Washington Academy. The assembly gave a board of trustees, to be appointed later, the "power and authority to fix on some convenient situation, where to establish the Academy, and to contract for erecting the necessary buildings," as well as the power to "engage a president and professors, and all other officers necessary for conducting the civil and literary concerns of the academy, and to displace and supersede them at pleasure." The anticipated board was also authorized to raise money for the academy by way of a lottery to bring in a sum not exceeding $5,000. None of these powers could be exercised right away, however, because the assembly did not name the trustees until it amended the original act on December 24, 1814. Those named included Lewis Sewall, James Caller, George S. Gaines, Joseph Phillips, Thomas Malone, Joseph Carson, Thomas B. Creagh, Benjamin S. Smoot, Reuben Saffold, Benjamin I. Biddill and John Dean—all influential citizens of Washington County. The act as amended required these trustees to meet in St. Stephens on the first Monday of February 1815.[15]

When the academy was eventually located within the town of St. Stephens, it apparently became known as the St. Stephens Academy instead of the Washington Academy. Historian William Brantley notes that the Mississippi Territorial Assembly appropriated $500 to a St. Stephens Academy in 1816 and postulated that it must have been for the original academy since he noted that there was no record of any academy by the name of St. Stephens being chartered by the assembly before 1816. The academy later became the subject of legislation by the new Alabama Territorial Assembly on February 7, 1818, when it passed an act bringing the St. Stephens Academy under its authority by incorporating its president and trustees and giving them broad powers to "better regulate" it. The following persons were named as trustees: Silas Dinsmoor, Samuel Smith, George Buchanan, Benjamin S. Smoot, Lemuel J. Alston, H. Mayhew, Mathew D. Wilson and Abner S. Lipscomb.[16]

In addition to having the first school in Alabama, St. Stephens was also home to one of Alabama's first newspapers. It was called the *Halcyon and Tombeckbe Public Advertiser* and was first published in the spring of 1815 by Thomas Eastin, who had found a damaged press and some type in the cantonment at Mount Vernon while serving under General Jackson as a division quartermaster. The *Halcyon* is believed to be surpassed by only the *Mobile Centinel* [*sic*], published at Fort Stoddert in 1811; the *Mobile Gazette*, published in Mobile in 1812; and the *Madison Gazette*, published in Huntsville in 1812. Eastin was later selected as the official publisher for the Alabama Territorial Assembly. As a leading citizen of St. Stephens, he was a member of St. Stephens's Masonic Lodge along with such luminaries as Governor Israel Pickens, Colonel Silas Dinsmore, Thomas Malone, J.F. Ross, Daniel Coleman, John Womack, W.D. Gaines, James Roberts, James K. Blount, Ptolemy Harris, F.S. Lyon, Micajah Brewer and John F. McGrew.[17]

As statehood approached, the soon-to-be territorial capital of Alabama was still a rough and primitive village in the wilderness of the Tombigbee region. The area in and around Mobile was described by Alabama's first attorney general, Henry Hitchcock, upon his arrival from Vermont in 1817 as "a rude place—200 miles from civilization, surrounded by Indians. Isolated from the world, it was the logical refuge of rogues fleeing from justice." Hitchcock described the local inhabitants as "rough and disagreeable."[18]

Despite the remoteness and coarseness of the area, St. Stephens was primed to become the capital of the Alabama Territory. It was in a strategic location at the head of navigation of the Tombigbee River, it was the county seat of the largest county in the Alabama section of the Mississippi Territory, it was the center of population in the lower Tombigbee region and it had the distinction of building the first school in what would become the state of Alabama. Huntsville's *Alabama Republican* reported on September 30, 1817, that the "town of St. Stephens, at the head of ship navigation of the Tombigbee, is advancing with a rapidity beyond that of any other place, perhaps in the western country." The Huntsville newspaper further noted

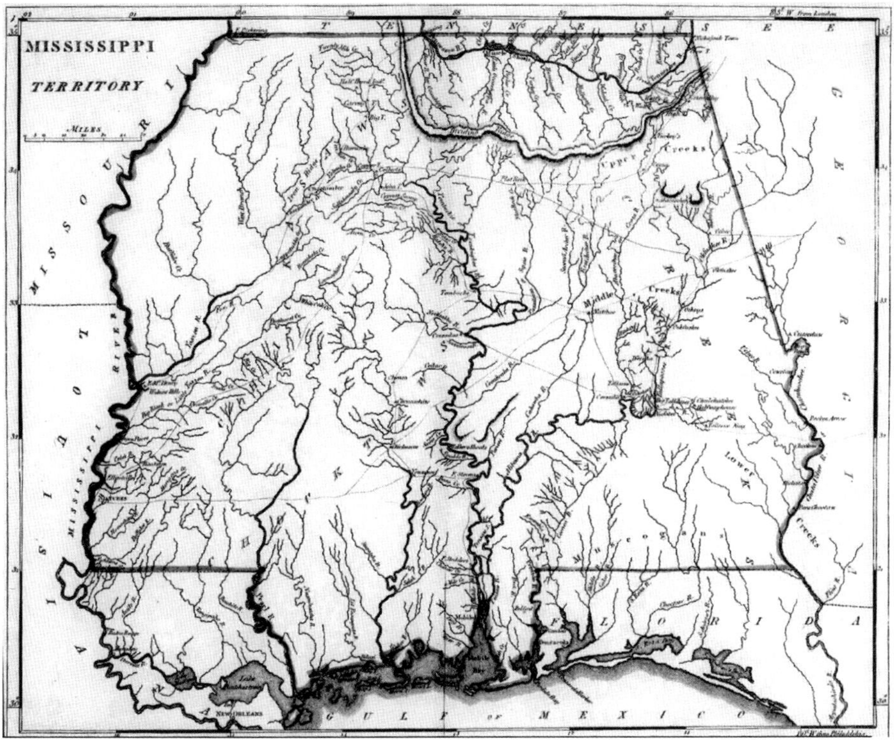

Map of Mississippi Territory. *Mississippi Territory (Sallus 1814), courtesy of the Birmingham (Alabama) Public Library.*

that St. Stephens had at least thirty new houses, many of which "would vie with those generally built in the United States"; an academy with two teachers and approximately seventy students; a steamboat at its dock that could run to New Orleans or as high up the Alabama River as Fort Claiborne; and merchandise annually amounting to not less than $500,000.[19]

Capital of the Alabama Territory (1817–1819)

Those in the western section of the Mississippi Territory who supported the admission of two states rather than one finally prevailed on March 3, 1817, when Congress passed an Enabling Act allowing the westerners to adopt a constitution and to be admitted to the Union separately from the eastern

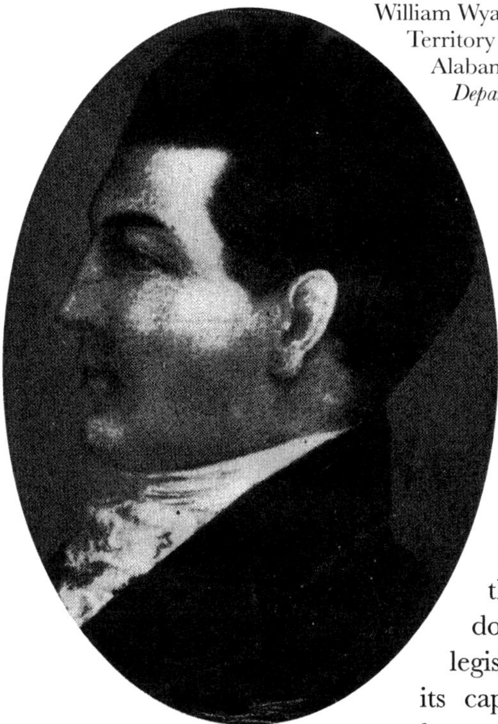

William Wyatt Bibb, governor of the Alabama Territory and first governor of the state of Alabama (1781–1820). *Courtesy Alabama Department of Archives and History.*

section. Accordingly, Mississippi was admitted to the Union as the nation's twentieth state by joint resolution of Congress on December 10, 1817. With Mississippi's admission to the Union, Alabama became its own territory, with St. Stephens as its capital "until it shall be otherwise ordered by the legislature thereof." Thus, the door was left open for the territorial legislature to change the location of its capital if sentiment favored such a change. The act creating the Alabama Territory gave the president of the United States the power to appoint a governor and a secretary of state. Accordingly, President James Monroe appointed William Wyatt Bibb, a former United States senator from Georgia, as the governor of the new territory and Henry Hitchcock as its secretary. The act further provided that "the governor to be appointed…shall immediately after entering into office convene at the town of St. Stephens such of the members of the legislative council and House of Representatives of the Mississippi Territory, as may then be the representatives from the several counties within the limits of the Territory to be established by this act." These members would constitute the legislative council and House of Representatives for the new Alabama Territory and would remain in power for so long as the term for which they were chosen or until Congress provided otherwise.[20]

In accordance with Congress's mandate, the members of the new territorial legislature convened in the town of St. Stephens on January 19, 1818, where they met in two rooms of Douglas's Hotel, located on High Street, which faced toward the Tombigbee River. In its initial session, the House of Representatives, consisting of twelve members, selected Gabriel

Moore, a native of North Carolina representing Madison County, as its Speaker. The council, or senate, had but one member due to the death and resignation of the other two members. That member, James Titus, who also represented Madison County, nevertheless met and conducted business. On January 20, 1818, the assembled representatives and sole council member listened to a written message from Governor Bibb, who extolled the qualities of the new Alabama Territory as "[a]mple in extent, abounding in navigable waters, and rich in the advantages of soil and climate." He further predicted that it would not be long before the "haunts of the savage will become the dwelling place of civilized man, and the forests of the wilderness be converted into fruitful fields." Once beyond these platitudes, Governor Bibb got down to specifics, urging that the legislature concentrate on education and internal improvements and pass an act authorizing that a census be taken prior to the next session of the legislature. During this session, the members selected John McGrew as the first representative from the Alabama Territory to the U.S. Congress. The members of the legislature also nominated six persons to be considered by the president of the United States, three of whom were to be selected by him for members of the legislative council. The persons nominated were George Phillips, Joseph Howard, Matthew Wilson, Joseph P. Kennedy, John Gayle and Reuben Saffold. Of these, the president chose Phillips, Wilson and Gayle.[21]

Soon after Governor Bibb's address, the members of the General Assembly quickly went to work in their first session, passing over fifty laws and resolutions that readied the territory for statehood. In response to Governor Bibb's emphasis on education and internal improvements, the assembly enacted measures that benefited St. Stephens. As previously seen, the St. Stephens Academy was incorporated, and its trustees were given broad authority to make regulations for the operation of Alabama's first school. The trustees were also given the authority to solicit $4,000 by way of a lottery. On February 8, 1819, the *Halcyon* informed its readership of the history of the lottery and the amounts to be drawn in the upcoming weeks, culminating with the chance of winning $10,000 for a $10 ticket.[22]

With regard to internal improvements, one of the first acts passed in the first session of the assembly was an act to incorporate the St. Stephens Steam Boat Company. Incorporators included James Pickens, David File, Silas Dinsmoor, Henry Bright, Benjamin S. Smoot and Daniel B. Ripley. The St. Stephens Steam Boat Company had the distinction of building the first steamboat, appropriately named the *Alabama*, on the Tombigbee River, and it is believed that it also was the first such boat to ply Alabama's waters in 1818. Unfortunately, however, after steaming downriver from St. Stephens to Mobile, it did not have enough power to return upstream to St. Stephens. Two years later, the steamboat *Tensas* successfully made it upstream to Cahaba. In that same year, the *Tombeckbe*, built by J.H. Dearing & Co., was launched at St. Stephens "amid the shouts and huzzas of a large concourse of spectators." The *Halcyon* further reported that "[s]he glided beautifully and majestically into the river, without the least accident." With accommodations for thirty passengers, the *Tombeckbe* was scheduled to travel regularly from New Orleans to Tuscaloosa with stops at Mobile, Blakeley, Jackson and St. Stephens.[23]

Another action of the first session of the territorial assembly that had a direct impact on St. Stephens was an act to establish the Tombeckbe Bank, which was passed on February 13, 1818. The bank, to be located in St. Stephens, was to issue capital stock not to exceed $500,000. The initial directors were to be David File, James A. Torbert, Dennison Darling, Thomas I. Strong, Israel Pickens, James G. Lyon, Jack F. Ross, William Crawford, Abner Smith Lipscomb, William D. Gaines, Nathan Whiting, Thomas Crowell and George Buchanan. Israel Pickens, a register in the land office and a future governor of the state of Alabama, was the first president of the Tombeckbe Bank. The bank proved to be a success under Pickens's skillful management. By arranging to have one of the bank's agents serve as the cotton factor for an overwhelming majority of the cotton produced in the area, Pickens was able to maintain the bank's solvency and to continue to provide specie during the bad times of the Panic of 1819. According to an account by Mary Welsh, however, the bank "was suddenly terminated by a robbery, which caused a wild and widespread tumult at the time. But the guilty party was never discovered, and a mystery still shrouds the robbery."[24]

In other action of more widespread significance, the territory's first legislature established judicial districts; provided for the regulation of judicial proceedings; granted the governor power to organize a militia; modified existing boundary lines, creating new counties; provided for the taking of a census in anticipation of statehood; repealed the law against usury, which had been passed by the Mississippi Territorial Assembly in 1816; and authorized the Alabama Territory to purchase two-thirds of the stock of the Planters and Merchants Bank of Huntsville. Having enacted over fifty laws and resolutions in their first session during January and February 1818, there was now time for the legislators and state officials who remained between sessions of the territorial General Assembly to settle down in the town of St. Stephens.[25]

The St. Stephens that welcomed the new legislators and other state officers was yet a remote town in the Old Southwest. The town got mixed reviews from correspondents of the era. For example, in May 1819, a resident wrote to a friend in Boston that it was the "jumping off place of this world." A more graphic description was provided by a silversmith from North Carolina, who wrote to his family in 1820, "St. Stephens is a rough frontier town with streets full of hogs wallowing in mud holes, barrooms, drunkards lying in and out of doors, scarlet women, bloody fights, shootings and killings, gambling games going on day and night." He then informed his family, "To a man of refined sensibilities it cannot be stood, so I am going to Huntsville, Ala." A more charitable view of St. Stephens was provided in a June 29, 1818 letter from a North Carolinian in which he proclaimed that there was "an almost entire change in its inhabitants, changing the worst of men for a better class." He further portrayed the town as having "from 16 to 20 stores of merchandise some of which would vie with the best in Newbern or Raleigh, N.C." He further reported that St. Stephens had approximately five hundred houses, a printing office, a bank, an academy and a steamboat, called the *Alabama of St. Stephens*. A foreign visitor also reported, "St. Stephens is the prettiest town in the State of Alabama…Besides the spacious streets regularly laid out, many elegant houses, scattered among genteel declivities, and surrounded by trees, looking like villas, or ornamented cottages, delight the sight." He further observed that "the houses generally framed, some built of brick and stone, are in very good repair, and newly painted" and that "[a]lmost every house has a spacious garden which contributes at once to the embellishment of the town, and the comfort of its inhabitants." He closes his sketch of the town by asserting, "An air of ease and comfort prevails at St. Stephens and recommends it as a pleasant residence."[26]

The above visitor also indicated, "Excellent accommodations are afforded to travelers at the different taverns." In addition to Douglas's Hotel, in which the territorial legislature met, there were at least four other hotels and one boardinghouse: the Globe Hotel, the St. Stephens Hotel, the Planter's Hotel, the Gordy Hotel and Mrs. Rouse's Boardinghouse. The Douglas Hotel boasted that it had the "best accommodations the country affords." Its business was undoubtedly benefitted by the fact that it was the location of the territorial legislature. J.C. Dale, proprietor of the St. Stephens Hotel, however, stated in an advertisement that he, too, was "determined to continue to furnish the best the country affords," noting that "his Bar is supplied with the choicest liquors, and his Stables provided with good attendance and plenty of good Forage." Mrs. Rouse, proprietor of a smaller boardinghouse located next to the corner of High Street and Chambers Street, limited her clientele to "only a select few" young gentlemen.[27]

High Street, which looked toward the old fort and the Tombigbee River beyond, probably was the busiest location in St. Stephens. Historian William Brantley indicates that "[a]t right angles with High Street were Chambers, Orange, Spring, and Lime Streets, one of which became the highway to Mobile." The so-called Government Building (the Douglas Hotel), where the Alabama Territorial Assembly met, was on High Street facing away from the Tombigbee River and looking toward the Tombeckbe Bank located on the intersection of High Street and Lime Street. Among businesses also located on High Street were the land office, a dry goods store run by A.B. Carrington, a general store under the name of Coolidge & Bright, a general merchandise store run by Jack F. Ross, the law office of Samuel Boughton, a saddler's shop run by John McLaughlin, Alston's Stone Shop selling general merchandise, J. Downing's tailoring business, W&H Morrison

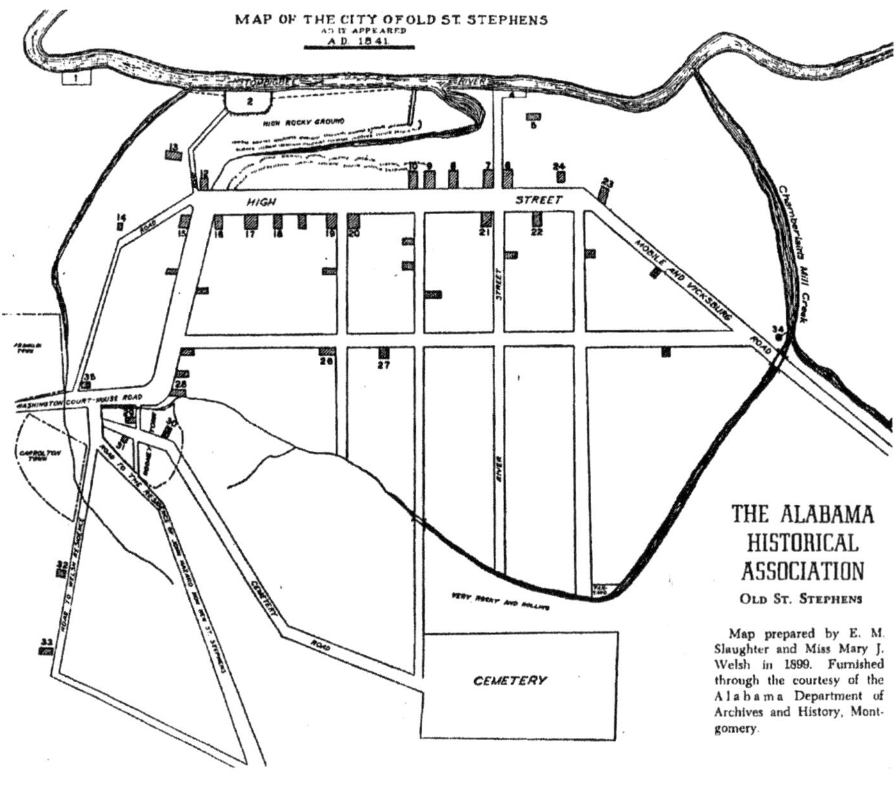

Map of Old St. Stephens. *Courtesy Alabama Department of Archives and History.*

Grocery, the law offices of F.H. Gaines and F.S. Lyon (1822) and a theater. Other commercial establishments in the town at large included cotton gin operations, a carriage-making business and various establishments selling such items as beaver hats, clothing, crockery, glassware, hardware, stationery, furniture, groceries and medicines. In addition to these businesses, others offered their wares as a sign and house painter, a barber, a baker and even a vendor of the *Edinburgh Encyclopedia*.[28]

With the influx of legislators and state officials, as well as the commercial expansion of this frontier capital in response thereto, members of the legal and medical professions were attracted to St. Stephens, where they hung out their shingles to practice law or medicine. A Dr. Archibald R. Woodson reportedly had settled in St. Stephens as early as 1818 and offered his services to the town's inhabitants and to those in the nearby vicinity. In 1819, a Dr. Bonnar was the proprietor of an apothecary's shop in a building opposite Coolidge & Bright's on High Street. An advertisement run in the local paper on June 3, 1820, by John St. John and Samuel St. John, doing business as S. St. John & Co., indicated that "advice to country people at all times will be given to those who purchase Medicines, if required, gratis; all calls in the Practice of Physics, Surgery and Midwifery will be strictly attended to." According to historian William Brantley, Dr. John Meeker "was the foremost physician of the town." Other physicians practicing in and around St. Stephens at various times included Dr. Thomas Dean, Dr. Samuel S. Houston, Dr. Middleton Dougherty, Dr. Joseph Huger and Dr. James G. Hawkins, who was the last physician in Old St. Stephens.[29]

Members of the legal profession who were attracted to St. Stephens in its zenith included Samuel Boughton, Morrison Hunter, George F. Salle, A.G. Ruffin, Reuben Saffold, Henry Hitchcock, William Crawford, John Gayle, F.H. Gaines and F.S. Lyon. Of these early Alabama lawyers, several had very distinguished and high-profile careers. Reuben Saffold, a veteran of the Creek War of 1813–14, was a member of the territorial legislature in 1818, a delegate to the Alabama Constitutional Convention of 1819 and eventually the chief justice of the Alabama Supreme Court. Henry Hitchcock, a native of Vermont and the grandson of Ethan Allen, was appointed as the secretary of the Alabama Territory in 1817, was a delegate to the Alabama Constitutional Convention in 1819, won election as the state's first attorney general, authored the first book published in Alabama, received appointment as a United States district attorney and served on the Alabama Supreme Court as both an associate justice and chief justice. John Gayle was Alabama's seventh governor and also served in the U.S. Congress, the state legislature and on the federal bench. Francis

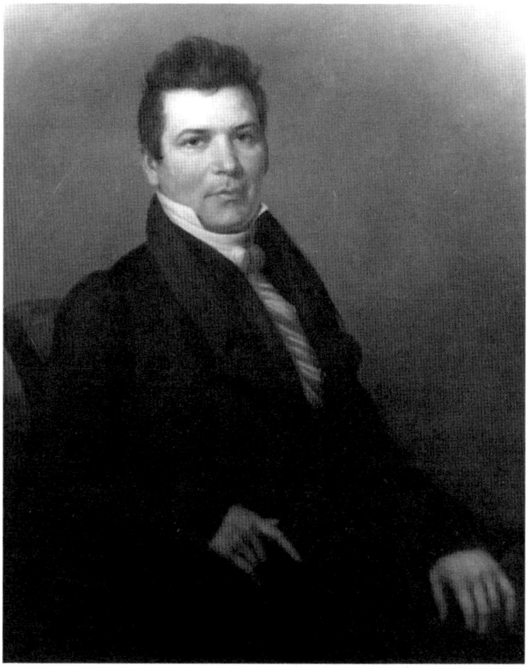

William Crawford (1784–1849) served as Alabama's first U.S. attorney, as president of the Tombeckbe Bank in St. Stephens and as Alabama's second federal judge. *Courtesy Alabama Department of Archives and History.*

S. Lyon worked in Alabama's first bank at St. Stephens in 1817 before practicing law in Demopolis, serving in the state senate in the mid-1830s and in the U.S. Congress from 1835 until 1839. In 1845, Lyon was also one of the commissioners to adjust claims against the state's banks placed in liquidation. William Crawford served as Alabama's first federal district attorney (United States attorney) in 1817, as president of the Tombeckbe Bank in St. Stephens in 1818 and as Alabama's second federal judge in 1826.[30]

Other prominent citizens of St. Stephens included Israel Pickens, first president of the Tombeckbe Bank and Alabama's third governor; Thomas Eastin, editor of the *Halcyon* and official publisher for the Alabama Territorial Assembly; Jack F. Ross, a legislator and state treasurer; George Strothers Gaines, Indian factor and later secretary and cashier of the Tombeckbe Bank; and Lewis Sewall, Alabama's first poet. Lewis Sewall, also an official in the St. Stephens Land Office, was publically accused by James Caller of embezzling funds from the land office. In retaliation for this accusation, Sewell wrote a satirical account of Caller's embarrassing defeat by the Creeks at Burnt Corn Creek in southwest Alabama during the Creek War of 1813–14. The work, entitled *The Last Campaign of Sir John Falstaff the II; or, the Hero of the Burnt-Corn Battle, A Serio-Comic Poem*, was published in 1815 and is believed to be the first work of literature published in the Mississippi Territory.[31]

Despite the rugged frontier nature of the town, St. Stephens was able to attract a number of traveling theater groups that generally appealed to all of the town's socioeconomic classes. St. Stephens's location at the head of navigation of the Tombigbee River made it relatively easy for traveling performers to get to. On January 18, 1819, the *Halcyon* gave notice of the upcoming performance of the comedy entitled *The Point of Honor* and a farce entitled *Fortunes Frolic*, both to be performed at the "New Theater." On May 24, 1819, the Thespian Company presented *She Stoops to Conquer* and the *Tragic Burlesque Opera of Bombastes Furioso*. The *Halcyon* advertisement for these performances noted: "Admittance is $1.00; performance begins promptly at 7:30 p.m.; and smoking in the theater [is] positively forbidden." Another traveling theater company, Messrs. Hunter, Jones & Drummond from the Virginia and New Orleans Theater, came to St. Stephens in April 1820 to perform a "gentlemen's Celebrated Comedy of *The Review or The Wag of Windsor* and the Laughable Piece called the *Weathercock or Love Alone Can Fix Him* with songs, recitations, etc." A local company, the Thespian Society of St. Stephens, took to the stage in August 1820 to perform the comedy *The Day After the Wedding, or a Wife's First Lesson*.[32]

Surprisingly, horse racing was more associated with the gentlemanly elite of the period than the theater, which appealed more generally to all of the socioeconomic classes. In November 1818, the *Halcyon* announced that the Pebble Spring Jockey Club Races would commence on the third Thursday in December "over one of the handsomest Turfs in the country (two miles south of town)." The first day of this particular session consisted of a three-mile run with a repeat; the second day consisted of a one-mile run with a repeat. The races were to be run in accordance with the rules of the club established by its president, Thomas H. Douglas, who was also the proprietor of Douglas's Hotel. Jeffrey C. Benton, who has written about leisure time in the antebellum period, postulates that racing meets such as these in antebellum Alabama "provided opportunities to display the exaggerated manners of the elite, especially for those with social aspirations." They also provided, in the tradition of the gentleman, opportunities to gamble and to enjoy the excitement of seeing the horses compete in what was to become America's first spectator sport.[33]

There were few additional entertainments for the residents of St. Stephens other than occasional holiday celebrations and balls. With regard to the Fourth of July celebration in 1819, for example, Thomas Eastin of the *Halcyon* reported, "Yesterday the 4th of July, coming on the Sabbath, no huzzas or rejoicings were heard, but this morning the day was ushered in by discharges from a small piece in town—a dinner at 2 o'clock—a play in the evening and tomorrow night a Ball at Mrs. Lindsay's." It is somewhat surprising that the celebration was delayed on account of the Sabbath in light of the fact that there were no regular religious services of any kind in the town, which had no church buildings or any regular "Minister of the Gospel."

On infrequent occasions, however, a minister riding the circuit would make arrangements to preach in St. Stephens, usually at someone's residence or at the theater where a small group of worshipers met sporadically. The theater also served as the site for a later Fourth of July celebration in 1822. The *Halcyon* reported, "The anniversary of our glorious independence was observed in this place with every mark of joy and exultation. The day was ushered in by a discharge from a field piece—at 12 o'clock a large concourse of the people of the town and its neighborhood assembled at the Theater, where the Declaration of Independence was read." A dinner followed that evening, presided over by Colonel Silas Dinsmoor and during which many patriotic toasts were made, including ones to George Washington, Thomas Jefferson, Andrew Jackson and the departed heroes of 1776 who "rest in their graves but their deeds are recorded in Heaven."[34]

One of the itinerant preachers who traveled through St. Stephens was Larenzo Dow. Dow, believed by many to be eccentric, was described by Thomas Eastin as wearing "his hair long or flowing, and his beard unshorn, in imitation of the Apostles." He further portrayed him: "His dress is mean, his voice harsh; his gesticulation and delivery ungraceful in the extreme and his whole appearance and manners are calculated to excite the curiosity and wonder of the hearers." Popular legend has it that Dow was dismayed at the lack of regular worship in St. Stephens and chastised the populace, which he called wicked and sinful, for frequenting the local taverns on the Sabbath rather than attending church. So goes the legend that the townspeople, not appreciative of Dow's holier than thou attitude, tarred and feathered him before sending him down the Tombigbee River on a raft. Reportedly, Dow then put a curse on St. Stephens with an admonition that the "bats and owls will inhabit the city and make it their home and pestilence will soon drive the inhabitants from the city." St. Stephens, indeed, would not survive long as a town, but its demise would be the result of worldly problems rather than due to a supposed curse cast on it by an eccentric itinerant preacher.[35]

St. Stephens Loses Its Status as Capital

At St. Stephens's zenith, the Alabama Territorial General Assembly met there again for the last time in November 1818. In the midst of dealing with the transition to eventual statehood, the assembly was presented with a sensitive issue when Mary Parham Moore, wife of Speaker of the House Gabriel Moore, sought a divorce and permission to revert to her maiden name. That petition was approved and enacted into law on November 17, 1818. A week earlier, the assembly had dealt with a much more momentous issue by approving a joint resolution formally petitioning Congress for statehood, which was promptly sent to Senator Charles Tait of Georgia to start the process of enacting an Enabling Act for the proposed state of Alabama. Probably the most important action taken by the assembly dealt with apportionment of the legislature. The legislation was a result of a power struggle between the northern counties, which favored including only the white population in determining apportionment, and the southern counties, which wanted to limit the number of representatives any one county could have. The southerners relented to the white population apportionment basis only when a rider was added to the bill designating Cahaba, located in Dallas County, where the Alabama and Cahaba Rivers converged, as the capital of the territory. The northerners, however, agreed to this only when they were successful in having Huntsville designated as a temporary capital of the territory "until suitable buildings and accommodations can be provided at the town of Cahawba."[36]

The designation of Cahaba as the future capital of the territory was the surprise result of astute political maneuvering by Governor Bibb that conflicted with the wishes of commissioners appointed by the first session of the territorial assembly "to examine and report to the Governor, the most eligible site for the Territorial Government, as near the center of the Territory as may be." Although the commissioners had recommended Tuscaloosa, Governor Bibb used his connections in Washington to secure passage of a bill that granted a free section of land for use as the state's seat of government and gave the governor the prerogative to select the site. Bibb, who favored the Alabama-Cahaba River basin as the site of government, chose a tract of land at the confluence of the Alabama and Cahaba Rivers. As we have seen, Governor Bibb then added a rider to the apportionment bill designating Cahaba as the new capital. Northern representatives who had favored Tuscaloosa nonetheless relented due to the fact that the tract of land designated by Governor Bibb was free—because they wished to avoid a gubernatorial veto of the apportionment bill that favored the northern counties and because they were successful in having Huntsville designated as the territory's temporary capital.[37]

The capital's departure was a death knell for St. Stephens. Only three years after its departure, the *Halcyon* editor Thomas Eastin expressed concern for the "declining condition of the town." In a March 1822 editorial concerning the status of St. Stephens, Eastin wrote, "Inhabitants of St. Stephens amount to

250–300. Several houses (some of them elegant buildings) are left untenanted. Its trade has declined." The Bank of Tombeckbe survived for a few more years, as did the St. Stephens Academy, which had between 40 and 50 students in 1822. However, just four years earlier, St. Stephens had a population of several thousand and an estimated five hundred houses. This rapid drop in population and in the number of residences foretold St. Stephens's ultimate demise. Mary Welsh, one of St. Stephens's former residents, summarized the perceived causes of its demise in addition to the loss of the seat of government. These included the "extension of navigation to points above," the "unhealthfulness of the locality" and the "Godlessness of its citizens." Her statement regarding Godless citizens was probably based on the legend of Larenzo's curse. Other more worldly causes—in addition to the loss of the capital, yellow fever epidemics and the extension of navigation beyond St. Stephens—included the loss of the Indian trading post to a locale upriver and Mobile's increasing importance after it was acquired by the United States in 1813. By 1833, St. Stephens was just a small village after many of its former inhabitants moved a couple of miles to the west, where they founded a community at a railroad crossroads that they named New St. Stephens. Others moved southward to Mobile and northward to the new capital at Cahaba. The town was abandoned to such an extent that by the time of the Civil War, it was a ghost town with its buildings falling into ruins and thick woods covering its former proud streets.[38]

Site of St. Stephens Today

Today, the site of Old St. Stephens is one of the most important archaeological sites in the state. In 1988, the St. Stephens Historical Commission was incorporated to sponsor and promote historical research and archaeological studies at Old St. Stephens. Perhaps the most important research project to date with regard to St. Stephens was undertaken by Jacqueline Matte, author of the *History of Washington County: First County in Alabama*, assisted by local genealogists Doris Brown and Barbara Waddell. Funded by a grant from the Alabama Humanities Foundation Matte, Brown and Waddell compiled land deeds, tax records, estate records, descriptions of St. Stephens, Indian agents' correspondence and excerpts from the *Halcyon and Tombeckbe Public Advertiser*. This compilation, entitled *Old St. Stephens: Historical Records Survey*, was first published in 1997 and has become an invaluable resource for those interested in Alabama's first capital. In 1999, the St. Stephens Historical

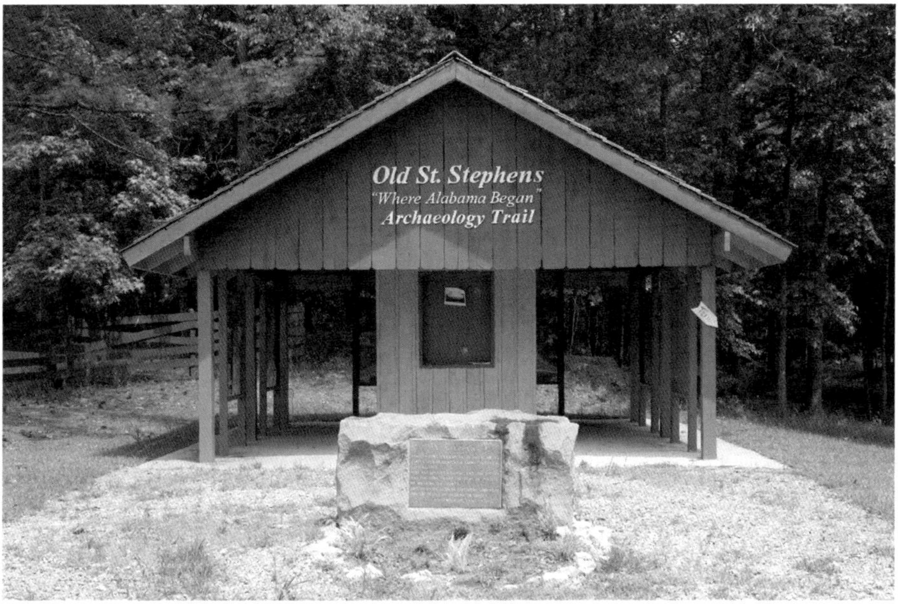

Contemporary photograph of Old St. Stephens's Archaeology Trail. *Library of Congress.*

Commission received a grant from the Alabama Historical Commission to continue archaeological studies of Old St. Stephens. Since the late 1990s, University of South Alabama archaeologist George Shorter and many volunteers have been involved in excavating the site of the old Globe Hotel and its attendant slave quarters, kitchen and stables. Items unearthed over the years include foundation remains, glass and ceramic fragments, nails, hinges and iron stirrups. Although now retired, Shorter continues to direct the ongoing digs at the site. In addition to the important historical and archaeological aspects of the site, modern visitors to the St. Stephens Historical Park now enjoy fishing, camping, biking, bird watching, horseback riding and hiking.[39]

St. Stephens's reign as Alabama's first seat of government, although short, was significant in that it involved the formation of Alabama's territorial government in anticipation of eventual statehood. Between 1817 and 1819, St. Stephens was buzzing with activity: it became the seat of Washington County, a federal land office was located there, it was home to the Choctaw Trading House, its other businesses were thriving, its population was increasing, it had the first school in the state's history, it had one of Alabama's first newspapers, steamboats plied the waters between it and New Orleans, its hotels and taverns were generally full, theatrical groups performed and horses raced to provide amusement for its citizens. Despite its rapid decline after the capital left, St. Stephens will forever be remembered as "Where Alabama Began."[40]

Chapter 2
Huntsville

Temporary Capital (1819)

Early Days (1805–1818)

Approximately three hundred miles to the north of St. Stephens, the emerging town of Huntsville in the great bend area of the Tennessee River was poised to become Alabama's temporary capital in 1819. Although the town of Huntsville was not incorporated until December 9, 1811, Madison County had been created on December 13, 1808, and settlers had been in the Huntsville area since 1805, some six years after the surrender of Fort St. Stephens by the Spanish to the United States. Huntsville was centrally and strategically located in the fertile Tennessee Valley and was the only town of any significant size in north Alabama.[41]

The Tennessee Valley in north Alabama had opened up for settlement after the Chickasaw and Cherokee Nations relinquished their claims to the area in treaties concluded in 1805 and 1806. A few years prior to these cessions, the first white settlers entered that part of the great bend of the Tennessee River that would become Madison County. James Ditto is believed to have been the first such settler, as early as 1802, to arrive in the area, where he established a ferry and trading post on the north bank of the Tennessee River then known as the Chickasaw Old Fields, later known as Whitesburg or Ditto's Landing. In 1805, John Hunt, a native of Virginia and a former sheriff in Tennessee, settled in the area that would become the city of Huntsville, where he built a cabin for his family on a bluff overlooking a natural spring he dubbed "Big Spring." A future senator from Alabama, John

Williams Walker enthusiastically boasted that "Huntsville is situated around the finest spring in the world; the spring forms a semicircle 100 feet wide, and at trivial expense the stream can be made navigable for batteux to the Tennessee River; which is only ten miles distant." Anne Royall, a journalist visiting the South, described the spring "as a great natural curiosity." She also related that Hunt had to spend much of his time fending off rattlesnakes, reporting that these snakes "had entire possession of the Bluff at the Spring. Thousands of them, it appears, were lodged amongst the rocks, and the Captain would shoot hundreds of a day."[42]

As a result of the petitions of an increasing number of settlers in the great bend country, the governor of the Mississippi Territory created Madison County, named for then secretary of state James Madison, by an executive order on December 13, 1808. At this time, there were approximately 2,500 settlers, including 2,223 whites and 322 slaves, in the newly created county. In order to increase the population further, in 1809, the United States government opened up land in Madison County for public sale. The first such sale was conducted on August 7, 1809, at the Public Land Office in Nashville. By October 1809, approximately 24,000 acres had been gobbled up at a total cost in excess of $67,000. Included within these sales were a number of acres surrounding Big Spring, by then known as Hunt's Spring. This purchase was made by Leroy Pope, a wealthy Georgia planter, in the hopes of having the area around the spring become the county seat of Madison County. Subsequent sales resulted in a total of 126,035 acres within Madison County being sold by the fall of 1811 just after the U.S. Land Office in Nashville moved to Huntsville.[43]

On February 27, 1809, the Mississippi territorial legislature bestowed on Madison County the necessary structure for a county government, primarily by directing the establishment of circuit and county courts, as well as by extending the territory's militia laws to the new county. This same legislation appointed a commission to select a site for the county's seat of government. At the recommendation of this commission, on July 5, 1810, the area surrounding Hunt's Spring was designated as the county seat of Madison. Leroy Pope, who was part of a wealthy group of planters and powerful politicians from the Broad River region in Georgia, had acquired most of this acreage by ousting older squatters from the land. Using his political influence, Pope was then successful in having the legislature mandate that the town be named Twickenham in honor of the estate of English poet Alexander Pope. This was viewed as "high-handed" by the older settlers of more modest means, and thus, the town's name was made an issue in the next

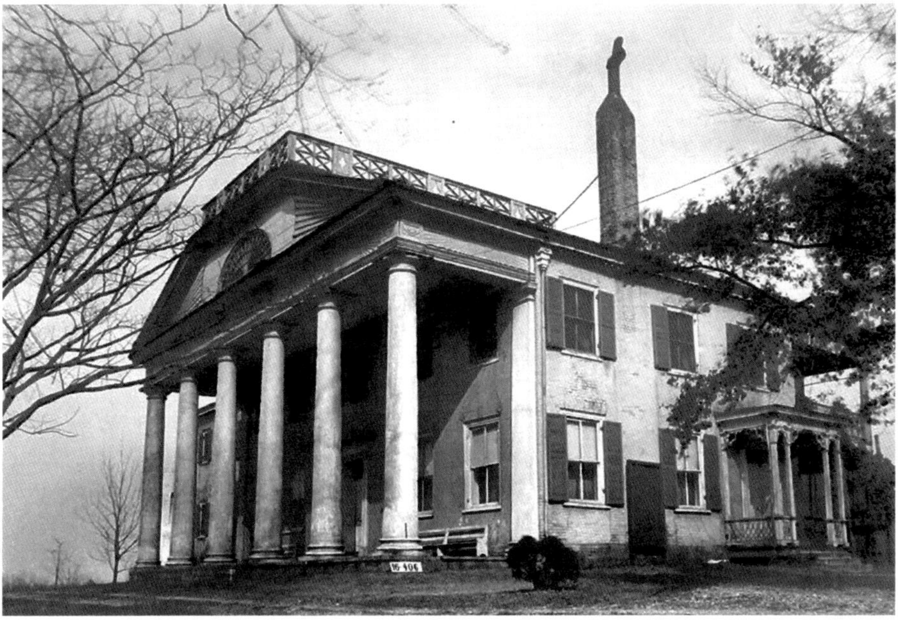

Pope Mansion, built in 1814. Leroy Pope (1765–1844), a leading citizen and landowner, is considered the "Father of Huntsville." *Library of Congress, Prints & Photographs Division HABS ALA,45-HUVI,4--.*

elections to the legislature. As a result, two out of the three candidates put up by Pope's Georgia faction were defeated, and the county's new legislative delegation quickly had the town's name changed to Huntsville, in honor of John Hunt, who was one of the original squatters in the area. On December 9, 1811, the new town of Huntsville was incorporated by the legislature, some eight years prior to the capital temporarily coming to town.[44]

After Huntsville was incorporated on December 9, 1811, it began a transformation from a rugged frontier settlement to a more sophisticated urban center. By 1816, Huntsville's public square consisted of a courthouse in its center surrounded by a market house, the Planters and Merchants Bank of Huntsville, twelve stores, several lawyers' offices and a wooden jail. In a letter dated January 1, 1818, journalist Anne Royall reported that "[t]he town stands on elevated ground, and enjoys a beautiful prospect." She estimated that there were approximately 260 houses in Huntsville at that time, mostly built of brick. As for these houses, she proclaimed, "The workmanship is the best I have seen in all the states; and several of the houses are three stories high, and very large." As for the area surrounding Huntsville, she declared, "The land around Huntsville, and the whole of Madison County, of which it is the capital, is rich and beautiful as you can imagine; and the appearance of wealth would baffle belief." Finally, regarding the citizens of Huntsville, she indicated that they were "gay, hospitable, and live in great splendor. Nothing like it in our country."[45]

As the population increased, there was an increasing need for a school in Madison County. Recognizing this need, in 1812, the Mississippi territorial legislature incorporated the Green Academy in Huntsville, which was built on the north side of present-day Clinton Avenue between Calhoun Street and White Street. A local paper stated that it would be in a "pleasant grove, on a beautiful eminence only a quarter of a mile from the heart of town." It was chartered as a tax-exempt school, and its trustees were authorized to raise up to $4,000 by way of a lottery. The Green Academy became the second educational academy to be incorporated in what was to become Alabama. The first academy to be incorporated was the Washington Academy in St. Stephens. In 1812, the Huntsville-based *Madison Gazette* became the second newspaper published in the Alabama portion of the Mississippi Territory. This weekly, founded by William W. Parham, was taken over by T.B. Grantland in 1816 and was given a new name, the *Huntsville Republican*. As for religious institutions, Anne Royall reported that there was no church in town but that services were held in the courthouse. Although there were no churches, there was a whiskey shop and even a bowling alley. Another one of Huntsville's more secular landmarks was the Green Bottom Inn and Racetrack. The Green Bottom Inn was one of Huntsville's earliest inns, located on Meridian Street where Alabama A&M University now stands. It—along with the Green Bottom Racetrack—was built in 1815 by John Connely, a Revolutionary War veteran. A frequent visitor of the inn, where "he raced his horses and fought his cocks," was General Andrew Jackson. Among other distinguished visitors to the inn was President James Knox Polk.[46]

In 1815, John Williams Walker reported to the U.S. secretary of the treasury, William H. Crawford, that there were five cotton gins within the immediate vicinity of Huntsville and another twenty within Madison County. He also asserted that the "average land in the county will produce 1,000 pounds of cotton to the acre and 800 bales will be this year's crop." In the winter of 1817–18, cotton prices were peaking at thirty cents a pound just as significantly more acreage was being allotted to the planting of cotton. This expansion of the cultivation of cotton resulted in almost doubling the slave population in the county between 1816 and 1820, an increase from below 30 percent of the total population to 47 percent. While cotton was

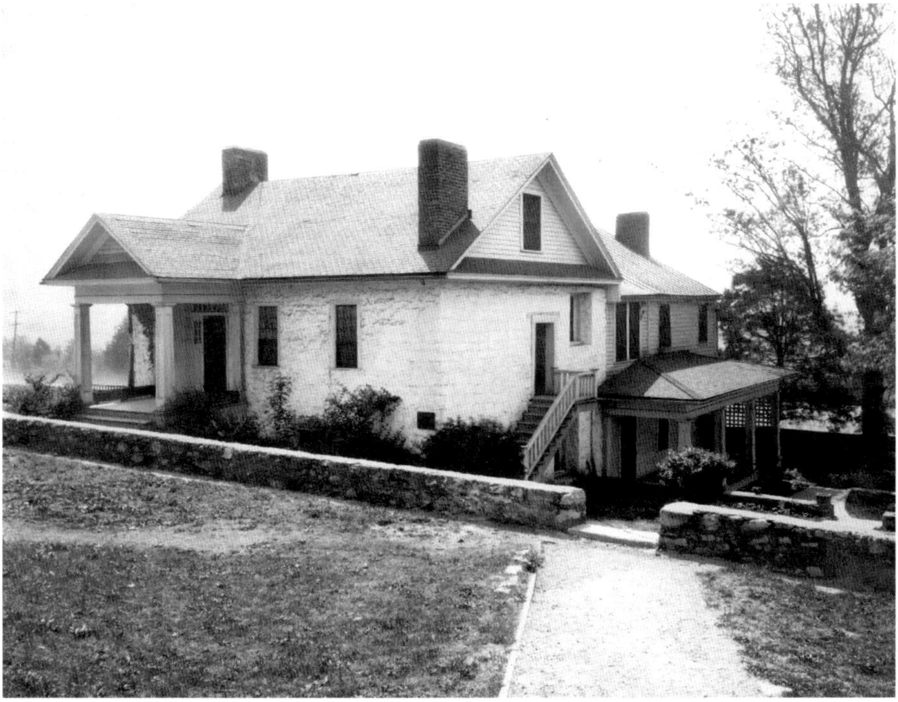

The Green Bottom Inn, built in 1815, was frequented by Andrew Jackson. He often stayed there and raced his horses. *Courtesy Huntsville–Madison County Public Library.*

booming, land values were skyrocketing. In Huntsville itself, for example, a lot on one of the corners of the public squire, which originally sold for $715, sold for $7,500 in 1816.[47]

Of further significance to Huntsville's development was the establishment of the Planters and Merchants Bank of Huntsville by the Mississippi territorial legislature on December 11, 1816. The commissioners who were appointed to open up the books for subscription to the capital stock of Alabama's first bank included Leroy Pope, John P. Hickman, David Moore, Benjamin Cox, John M. Taylor, John Fearn, Jessie Searcy, Clement C. Clay and John Williams Walker. The legislature authorized a capital stock of $500,000, divided into five thousand shares of $100 each. The bank opened for business on October 17, 1817, with Leroy Pope as its president. It was soon thereafter made the depository for the Huntsville Federal Land Office, which moved to Huntsville from Nashville in 1817. The bank, however, failed to make specie payments in 1820, which led to its ultimate closure in 1825.[48]

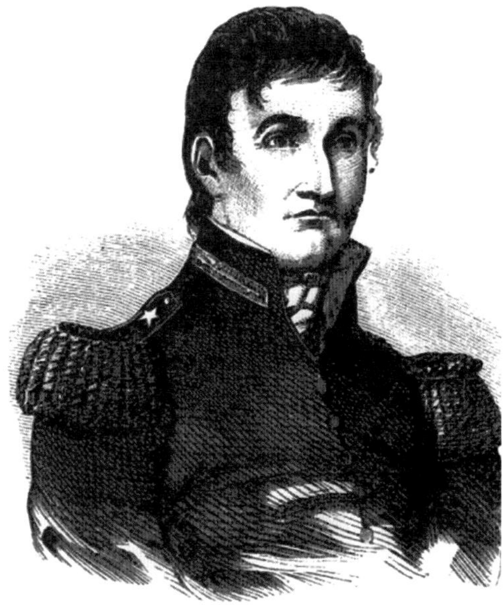

John Coffee (1772–1833), a colleague of General Andrew Jackson, founded the Cypress Land Company in which many prominent citizens of Huntsville invested. *Wikimedia Commons.*

The first census taken in Madison County in 1816 revealed a total population of 14,200. When the census was taken again in 1820, the total population had jumped up to 19,565. Of this number, 10,242 were white and 9,323 were African American slaves. Part of this increase was fueled by another land boom in 1818 in the Tennessee Valley, wherein $7 million worth of land was sold just west of Madison County on both sides of the Tennessee River. Land companies sprang up overnight to compete for the business of the settlers and speculators who came rushing in to purchase these newly opened lands. Land that sold for $2 an acre in 1809 was then selling for $10 to $20 dollars an acre in 1818. Early Huntsville historian Edward Chambers Betts asserted that these sales "created as great excitement as did the California gold fever in 1848–49." He stated further that "[b]idding at these sales were spirited, and the average price paid ranged from $50.00 to $54.00."[49]

One of the most lucrative land companies to take part in this boom was the Cypress Land Company, which was founded by John Coffee and James Jackson, who were colleagues of General Andrew Jackson. Investors included General Jackson and President James Madison, as well as leading citizens of Huntsville, such as future governor Thomas Bibb; president of the Planters and Merchants Bank of Huntsville Leroy Pope; and future U.S. Supreme Court justice John McKinley. The Cypress Land Company's most significant purchase was a tract of land consisting of 5,515 acres that would become the site of the town of Florence. General Jackson, who owned a few shares of stock in the Cypress Land Company, was able to purchase land from it at rock-bottom prices of two dollars an acre. This consisted of valuable cotton lands located at the head of the Elk River shoals in Lawrence County near Florence. With the aid of an overseer and sixty slaves at this

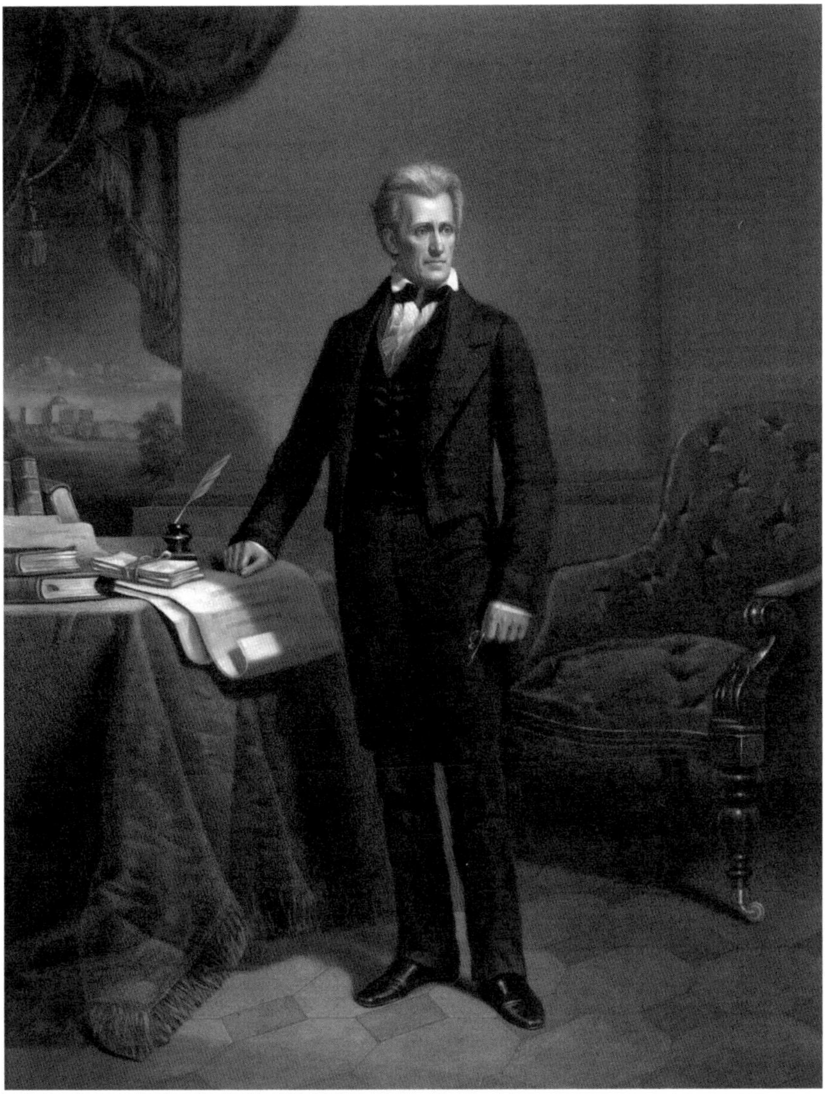

Andrew Jackson, a frequent Huntsville visitor, used his influence to acquire cheap land in north Alabama from the Cypress Land Company. *Library of Congress.*

site, Jackson ran a fully operational cotton plantation at a distance from his home at the Hermitage near Nashville.[50]

Historian Edwin Betts summed up the rapid development of Huntsville as follows: "The town was crowded with people; hotels were taxed to their utmost limit to lodge the throngs of transients; the bank itself was inadequate for the times, and could not care for the commercial interests for the community." As the town grew, its citizens and visitors traversed streets named for the nation's founding fathers, including George Washington, Patrick Henry, George Clinton, Thomas Jefferson, Benjamin Franklin, Albert Gallatin, James Madison, Nathanael Greene, Benjamin Lincoln and Horatio Gates. Two other streets were named for territorial governors David Holmes and Robert Williams. Parcels immediately surrounding Williams Street near the Big Spring had been purchased by Leroy Pope in August 1809 at a premium of twenty-three dollars per acre. Others residing in the Williams Street area at various times included John McKinley, Henry Minor and Thomas Bibb. On the other patriotically named streets were located many businesses, lawyers and doctors, as well as a two-story brick courthouse, a jail, a weekly newspaper, the Planters and Merchants Bank of Huntsville, the Green Academy, several religious assemblages, cultural venues such as the Thespian Society and the Haydn Society and a Masonic lodge that had first been established in August 1811. The December 25, 1819 issue of the *Halcyon* advertised performances of the Thespian and Haydn Societies. The

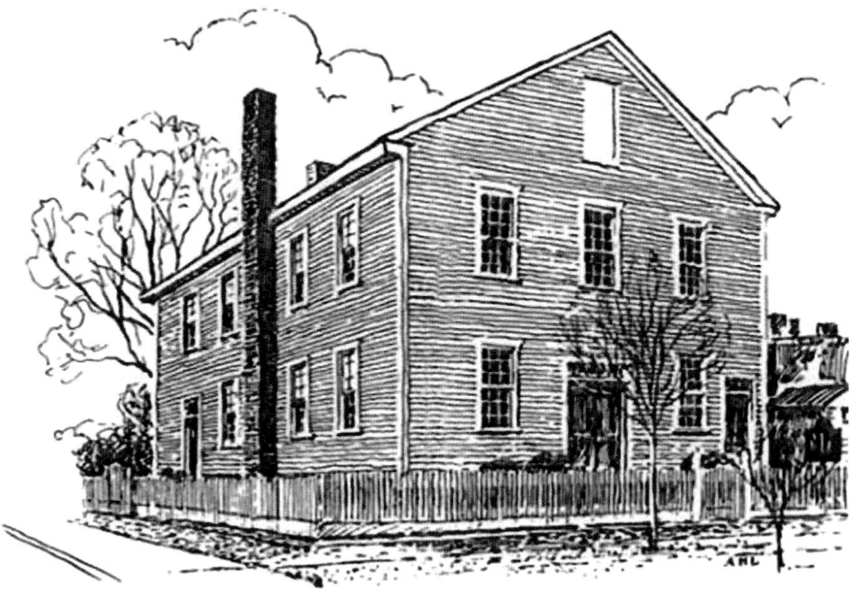

Constitution Hall, a former cabinet shop that housed the Constitutional Convention of 1819. *Courtesy Huntsville–Madison County Public Library.*

Huntsville Thespian Society announced that, due to bad weather on the previous evening, it was again performing *Heir at Law* and *Of Age Tomorrow*. Also, it was advertised that members of the Huntsville Haydn Society were to assist in a concert to be held at the Huntsville Inn, after which they were to provide music for dancing.[51]

Perhaps the most important structure in the town was a vacated cabinet shop, which would house the Constitutional Convention of 1819. After obtaining the titles of Cherokee and Chickasaw lands, two land booms, an invasion of Georgia planters, the creation of a local government and a commercial development related to rising cotton prices, Huntsville was ready to serve the future state of Alabama as its temporary capital while it hosted a convention to adopt a constitution necessary for Alabama's admission to the Union.

1819 Constitutional Convention and Temporary Capital

On March 2, 1819, the U.S. Congress passed an act authorizing the inhabitants of the Alabama Territory "to form for themselves a constitution and state government, and to assume such name as they may deem proper; and that the said territory, when formed into a state, shall be admitted into the Union, upon the same footing with the original states, in all respects whatsoever." As previously seen, representatives of the northern counties had been successful in securing Huntsville as a temporary capital while the town of Cahaba was being readied for the location of the "permanent" capital. Thus, the Enabling Act authorized delegates to meet in Huntsville on the first Monday of July 1819 to determine "whether it be, or be not expedient, at that time, to form a constitution and state government." Delegates from the territory's twenty-two counties were to be elected on the first Monday and Tuesday of May 1819. Madison County was allotted eight delegates, which was twice as many as any other county. This impressive delegation included John W. Walker, Clement Comer Clay, J.L. Townes, Henry Chambers, Lemuel Mead, Henry Minor, Gabriel Moore and J.M. Taylor. John W. Walker became the president of the Constitutional Convention and later became one of Alabama's first two senators; Clement Comer Clay became Alabama's eighth governor and served in the U.S. Senate; Henry Chambers was a physician and represented Alabama in the U.S. Senate; Henry Minor was a reporter for the Alabama Supreme Court and was an associate justice of that court; and Gabriel Moore was Alabama's fifth governor and served in the U.S. Congress.[52]

Only a month before the elected delegates were to convene in Huntsville to adopt a state constitution, the citizens of Huntsville were pleasantly surprised on June 1, 1819, with the unexpected arrival in their midst of President James Monroe. President Monroe was on a tour of the South purportedly to examine military fortifications, locate new sites for defensive posts, assess the area's improvement in agriculture and manufacturing and observe the conditions of local Indian tribes. Not surprisingly, it has been surmised that another object of his tour was to ingratiate himself with the citizens along his path so as to instill patriotic fervor amongst them and to curry their favor for his administration. When it was discovered that the president had arrived at a local inn, Clement Comer Clay quickly headed a committee to invite him to a public dinner to be held in his honor. The president readily accepted the invitation, and on June 2, 1819, at 4:00 p.m., approximately one hundred of Huntsville's leading citizens gathered to pay tribute to the fifth president of the United States. President of the dinner was Leroy Pope, assisted by Vice-Presidents Clement Comer Clay and Henry Minor. During the course of the dinner, more than twenty toasts were offered by various participants. Poignantly, President Monroe toasted the territory of Alabama: "May her speedy admission into the Union advance her happiness, and augment the national strength and prosperity." The next day, President Monroe headed for Nashville, and Huntsville's citizens turned their attention to the Constitutional Convention soon to convene in their town. A few weeks later, Huntsville's *Alabama Republican* reported the arrival of territorial governor Bibb in Huntsville. It further reported, "The Secretary of the Territory is daily expected and the public records, etc., have already arrived here, where they will remain while this place continues to be the seat of government."[53]

Of the forty-four delegates who assembled in Huntsville on July 5, 1819, about one-third of them were lawyers, four were planters, four were physicians, two were ministers, one was a merchant and the rest were not identified. Distinguished delegates outside of Madison County included Judge Harry Toulmin; William Rufus King, future U.S. senator and vice president; Israel Pickens, Alabama's third governor; and Reuben Saffold, future chief justice of the Alabama Supreme Court. Since there was no hall big enough to accommodate all of these distinguished delegates, they met in a vacant cabinet shop located at the corner of Franklin and Gates

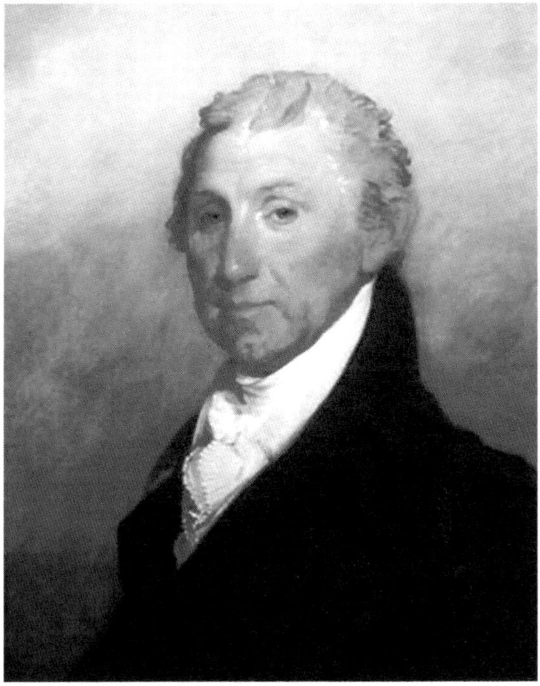

President James Monroe paid a surprise visit to Huntsville in June 1819, just months before he signed a resolution formally admitting Alabama into the Union. *Wikimedia Commons.*

Streets. The shop had been owned by cabinetmaker Walker Allen, who had recently died. The building was frequently rented out as an assembly hall and theater. As a matter of fact, in 1819, the Huntsville Thespian Society held its first performance in this building. Nearby in the same block were future Huntsville mayor John Boardman's print shop, Clement Comer Clay's law office, the federal land surveyor's office, a post office, Sheriff Stephen Neal's residence and the Huntsville Library, which was the first library in the state to be incorporated by the legislature on November 27, 1819.[54]

The first order of business for the Constitutional Convention was to elect a presiding officer. In a unanimous vote, Madison County's John W. Walker, who had been Speaker of the House of the last session of the General Assembly of the Alabama Territory, was given this honor. Madison County also provided the only other convention officers when the convention elected John Campbell as secretary and Daniel Rather as doorkeeper. After the election of these officers, President Walker briefly addressed the assembled delegates, expressing his desire that "our deliberations may terminate in the adoption of a constitution which will secure to [Alabama's] sons, to the remotest generations, the full enjoyment of the great blessings of life, liberty, and property." John Campbell, the convention's secretary, wrote to his father in Virginia that the "convention is composed of 44 members and I have never seen in any deliberative body for the numbers more urbanity and intelligence."[55]

The convention next appointed a Committee of Fifteen to write a draft of Alabama's proposed constitution. The committee was chaired by Clement

Comer Clay of Huntsville. The other appointed members were for the most part from the planter counties bordering the Tennessee, Tombigbee and Alabama Rivers and included John M. Taylor and Henry Chambers of Madison County, Israel Pickens and Henry Hitchcock of Washington County, John Murphy and John Watkins of Monroe County, Thomas Bibb and Beverly Hughes of Limestone County, William Rufus King of Dallas County, Arthur F. Hopkins of Lawrence County, Reuben Saffold of Clarke County, John D. Bibb of Montgomery County, Richard Ellis of Franklin County and George Phillips of Shelby County. An even more

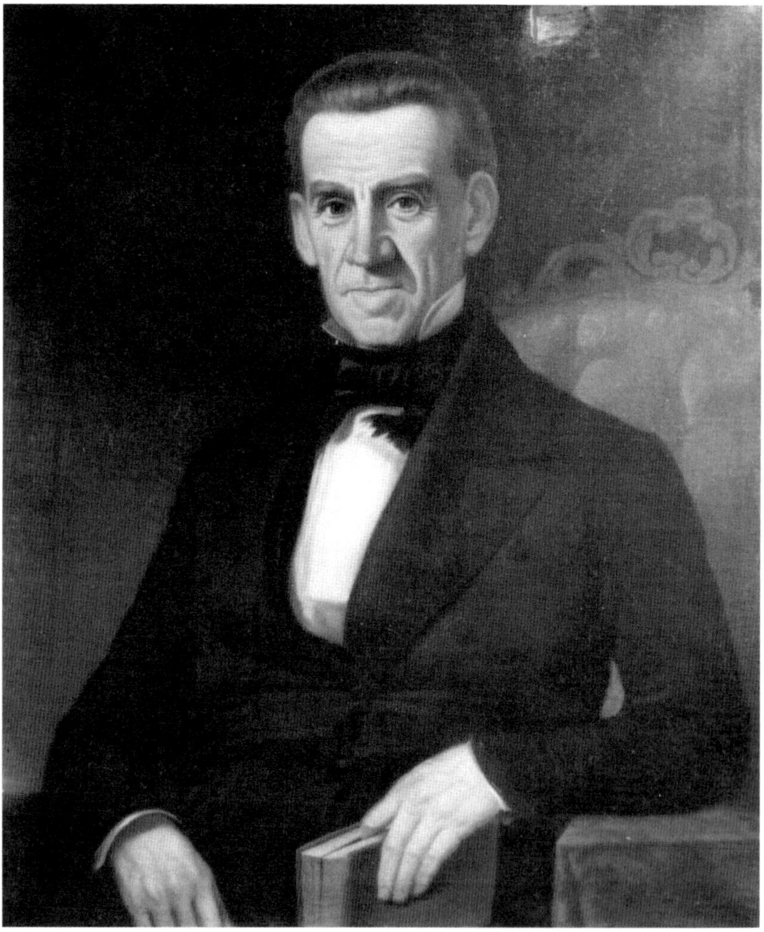

Clement Comer Clay (1789–1866) of Huntsville served in the Constitutional Convention, as Alabama's eighth governor and as a U.S. senator from Alabama. *Wikimedia Commons.*

select subcommittee of three was created to finalize the rough draft in a form presentable to the entire convention. This subcommittee consisted of William Rufus King, John M. Taylor and Henry Hitchcock.[56]

The final draft of the constitution was reported to the convention as a whole on July 13, 1819. After less than a month of deliberations and with just minor modifications, Alabama's constitution was adopted on August 2, 1819. The final product resembled the U.S. Constitution as far as providing the basic structure of government consisting of three branches—legislative, executive and judicial. Also, like the federal constitution, Alabama's contained a similar Bill of Rights set forth in Article I. Article II provided for the separation of powers between the branches of government, Article III set forth the powers of the legislative branch, Article IV set forth the powers of the executive branch and the state's militia and Article V provided for the judicial branch and the rules for impeachment. The final section contained general provisions pertaining to education, banks and slaves; rules for amending and revising the constitution; and a schedule for transforming from a territorial status to statehood. The constitution as adopted was considered liberal for its time primarily because it provided for universal white male suffrage, rejecting restrictive qualifications such as the ownership of property, taxpayer status or service in the state militia. However, the legislative branch was accorded disproportionate powers at the expense of the populace and the other branches of government. For example, the legislature was given the power to appoint most state officials rather than allowing them to be elected by the people.[57]

The section of the constitution pertaining to the legislature contained a provision relating to the location of the capital of the state that would be of benefit to Tuscaloosa in the future. As previously discussed, Governor Bibb had used his political influence in Washington to maneuver to have Cahaba chosen as the "permanent" capital instead of Tuscaloosa, as had been recommended by a special commission appointed by the first territorial legislature. In this regard, the constitution provided that the first session of the legislature would meet in Huntsville and thereafter in Cahaba until 1825. After the session in 1825, the representatives were given the authority to proclaim a new "permanent" capital without the concurrence of the governor. If a majority of the representatives did not name a new capital in 1825, the constitution provided that Cahaba would remain the state's capital by default.[58]

With the completion of their work, on August 2, 1819, all forty-four delegates signed Alabama's first constitution. President Walker said of the convention's work, "We have given the State of Alabama a Constitution—not indeed perfect... Yet emphatically republican and such as gives us a clear and indisputable title, to admission into the great family of the Union." The constitution was then enrolled, deposited with the secretary of state and transmitted to the U.S. Congress, where a resolution of admission into the Union was ultimately enacted. The constitution adopted by the Huntsville convention would remain in effect until it was replaced by a secessionist constitution in 1861.[59]

Huntsville's role in the establishment of the new state of Alabama was not yet completed. As soon as the Constitutional Convention's delegates headed home, campaigning began for seats in both houses of the General Assembly, as well as for governor, with elections set for these offices on the third Monday and Tuesday of September 1819. On those dates, twenty-two senators and fifty representatives were elected. Twenty-five of those had served in either the territorial assembly or the Constitutional Convention. At least three had served in the Revolutionary War. Also elected was Alabama's first governor, William Wyatt Bibb, who was finishing up his term as governor of the Alabama Territory. Bibb defeated Marmaduke Williams of Tuscaloosa, who was a former congressman from North Carolina. The election was relatively close due to a growing resentment of the Georgia faction and resentment as well for the manner in which Bibb had contrived to have the "permanent" capital located in Cahaba.[60]

On October 25, 1819, in anticipation of statehood, the recently elected representatives convened in Huntsville for the first session of the state of Alabama's General Assembly some six weeks before Alabama was officially admitted into the Union. For the first few sessions, the houses of the General Assembly met in separate locations. During that time, the House convened in the private residence of Irby Jones, while the senate was believed to be convening in the private residence of its doorkeeper, John K. Dunn. They both received approximately $150 for the use of their homes. The House later relocated to the first floor of the Madison County Courthouse. The senate remained where it was, but for joint sessions, both houses met in the courthouse. For forty-four days, the members of the General Assembly met in these locations and worked diligently to implement a government in accordance with the terms of the newly adopted constitution. To lead them in this important endeavor, the members of the House of Representatives elected James Dellet of Monroe County as Speaker of the House and Thomas Bibb, the governor's brother, as president of the senate. Governor Bibb sent a written message to the members of the General Assembly in which he

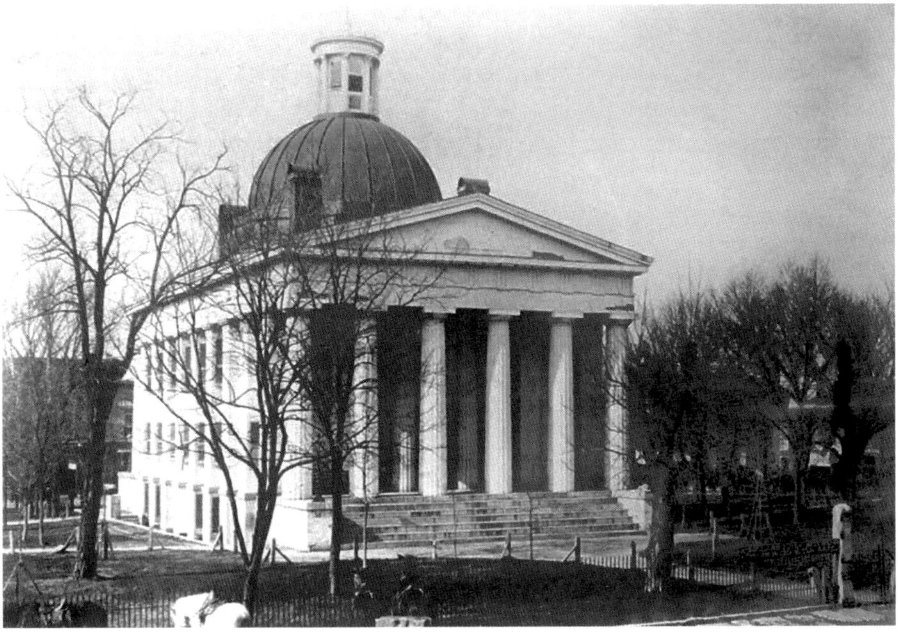

Second Madison County Courthouse in Huntsville, built in 1838. *Library of Congress, Prints & Photographs Division, HABS ALA,45-HUVI,10—1.*

stated that "your present meeting will form a memorial epoch in our history; chosen to perform the first acts of legislation, for the state of Alabama, you cannot estimate too highly the great interests committed to your charge, or the important consequences which may flow from your deliberations."[61]

Prior to turning their attention to the enactment of legislation, on October 28, 1819, the combined houses of the General Assembly undertook the important task of electing Alabama's first U.S. senators—John W. Walker of Madison County and William Rufus King of Dallas County. The sectional jealousy between north and south Alabama ensured that each section was represented in the Senate. After securing places to convene, organizing both of its houses and electing Alabama's first senators, the General Assembly got down to the business of passing seventy-seven acts and nine resolutions to make Alabama's government operational in accordance with the general outline set forth in the constitution. In this regard, courts were created, judges were elected, a militia was provided for, education was supported by the appointment of land agents to manage the lands donated by Congress for the benefit of schools, internal improvements were provided for with regard to public roadways and navigable waterways, a tax structure was created, new counties were created and towns were incorporated. Most of these enactments were accomplished before Alabama officially became a state on December 14, 1819. Thus, when the General Assembly adjourned its first

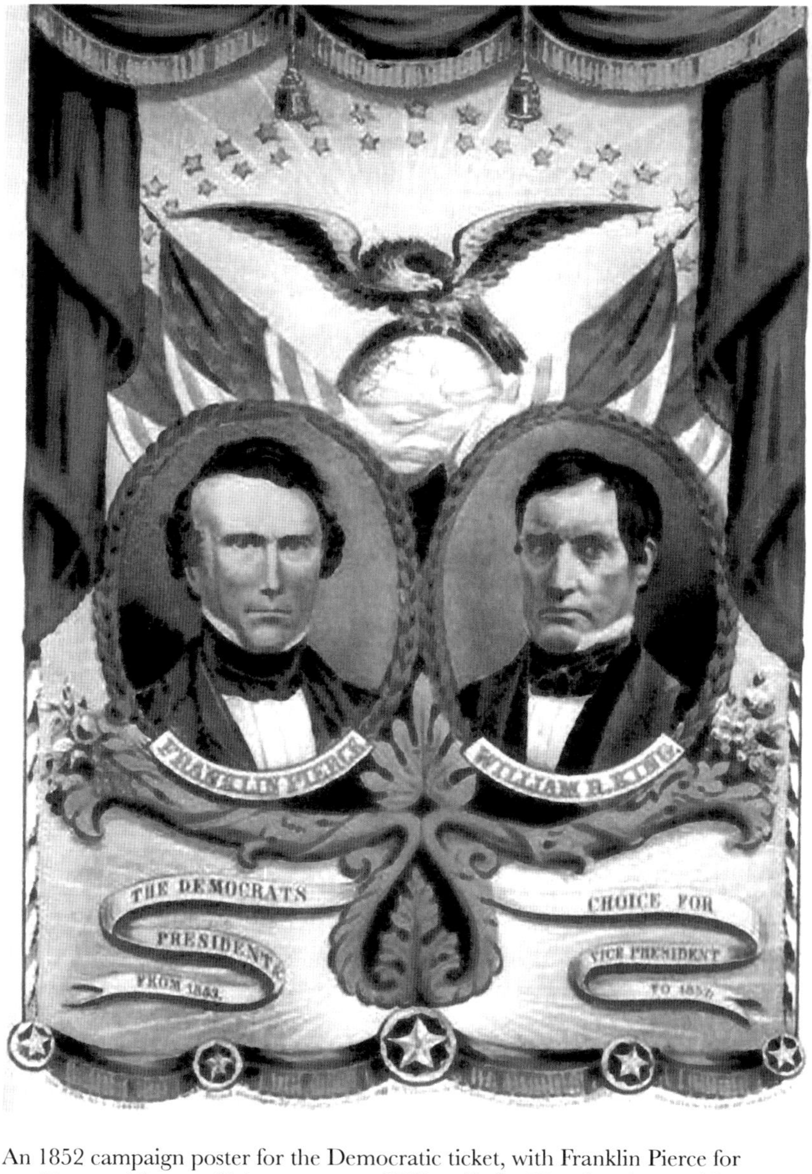

An 1852 campaign poster for the Democratic ticket, with Franklin Pierce for president and former Alabama senator William Rufus King for vice president. *Library of Congress.*

and only session in Huntsville on December 17, 1819, its members were unaware that President Monroe had signed the resolution formally admitting Alabama into the Union as the nation's twenty-second state.[62]

Prior to adjourning, the General Assembly had to authorize payment for the expenses it had incurred while in Huntsville and to prepare for its move to Cahaba. Expense items included printing services, railings for the lobby of the House, stationery, iron stoves, tables, benches and fifty chairs. The doorkeeper of the House was authorized to auction off items of furniture and to deposit the proceeds, less expenses, into the state treasury. With these matters attended to, state officials packed up and began their trek to Cahaba. The trip was not an easy one. From Huntsville, most of those traveling to Cahaba proceeded down the Tuscaloosa Road through Elyton in Jefferson County and, from there, to the falls of the Black Warrior River near Tuscaloosa. Moving on from this site of a future capital, travelers could either go down the Warrior and Tombigbee Rivers to the site of Alabama's original capital at St. Stephens, where they acquired new watercraft to ply up the Alabama River to Cahaba, or they traveled overland to Montevallo (then called Wilson's Hill), where they then took flat-bottomed boats from the falls of the Cahaba down that river to the site of the new capital.[63]

Post-Capital Development (1820–Present)

Huntsville, unlike St. Stephens, would not shrink into oblivion after the departure of the state's capital from its midst. Indeed, in time, Huntsville would become one of the most vibrant cities in the state. Immediately after the removal of the capital to Cahaba, however, Huntsville still exhibited some fairly rough and rowdy characteristics as demonstrated by a letter from a Huntsville citizen to a friend, dated August 16, 1820, in which he related two deaths by stabbing, a forgery and a horse theft within a short period of time. Despite instances of this nature, Huntsville was nevertheless quickly losing its backwoods character with a surge in its population from 1816 to 1820. The census taken in 1820 showed that Madison County had a total population of 19,565, which was an increase of 5,365 from that in 1816. Although the census did not reveal which portion of these numbers included residents of Huntsville, a census of just Huntsville was taken two years later, in 1822. This census revealed a total population for Huntsville of 1,306, of whom 833 were white, 448 were slaves and 25 were "free persons of color." According to Edward Chambers Betts, no town in Alabama had greater populations.[64]

With this increase in population, Huntsville's commercial development continued to evolve. Anne Royall, who had been absent from Huntsville for a few years, returned in 1822 and indicated that it had grown during her absence. "It's capital," she reported, "is considerable and the proprietors are thoroughgoing business men." Royall further regaled her correspondent with the additions she noticed upon her return, including two churches, a theater, more dwellings, two printing houses, sixteen stores, a fire engine, two academies, several "common schools," a "tolerable" library, several "fine" taverns and, several "Doggeries" (saloons). She also noticed that there were several "commission merchants," an auctioneer, twenty-one lawyers and eight physicians.[65]

Issues of Huntsville's *Alabama Republican* between 1820 and 1826 reveal a wide variety of local industries, including a beer brewery; a leather tannery; a watch and clock maker; manufacturers of boots, shoes, hats, candles and copper stills; and pumps to be used in connection with the waterworks system of Huntsville. During this period, the cultivation of cotton in the fertile Tennessee Valley was rebounding from the Panic of 1819, at which time cotton was selling at eighteen cents per pound, down from thirty-four cents per pound in 1818. Huntsville recovered from the Panic of 1819 and flourished between the 1830s and the 1850s, serving as the cotton and transportation center of the Tennessee Valley. With regard to transportation near Huntsville, in 1830, the legislature chartered the Tuscumbia Rail Company, one of the first railroads in America, which ran just two miles from the Tennessee River to the city of Sheffield. Just two years later, in 1832, the legislature chartered the Tuscumbia, Courtland and Decatur Railroad. This more serviceable line ran from Tuscumbia some forty-four miles to Decatur, bypassing the rapids on the Tennessee River at Muscle Shoals. To allow Huntsville residents to take advantage of this railroad, a stage line was established from Huntsville to the Tennessee River at Decatur. In 1854, transportation in the Tennessee Valley was bolstered when Huntsville became the headquarters of the Memphis and Charleston Railroad, the first railroad to link the Atlantic Ocean with the Mississippi River. With regard to the economic effect of "King Cotton," in 1832, the legislature chartered the state's first cotton mill, which contained three thousands spindles and one hundred looms, making it the first cotton manufacturing facility of any significance in the southeastern United States. It was located about ten miles northeast of Huntsville on the Flynt River. It was known as the Bell Factory

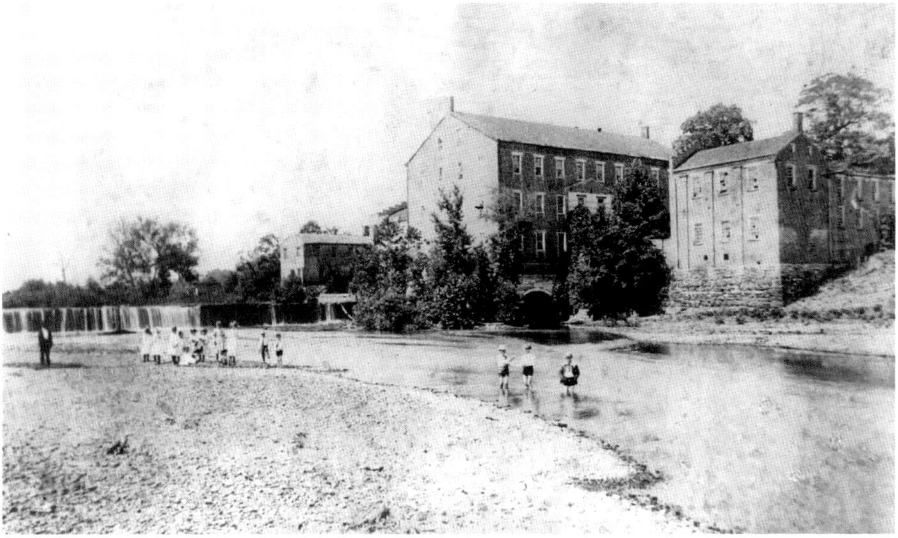

The Bell Factory, Alabama's first cotton mill, located about ten miles northeast of Huntsville, was chartered by the General Assembly in 1832. *Courtesy of Huntsville–Madison County Public Library.*

supposedly because of the fact that it had a bell that daily beckoned its slave labor force—consisting primarily of children between the ages of ten and fourteen—to work.[66]

According to Edward Chambers Betts, at the close of the period between 1820 and 1861, "Huntsville had three weekly papers: the *Huntsville Southern Advocate*, the *Huntsville Independent* and the *Huntsville Democrat*; four architects, twenty-four lawyers, three brick manufactories, three hotels, twelve doctors, a bank with a capital of $500,000; seven schools, two stage lines, two civil engineers, two saloons, one cotton and one woolen manufactory, one flour mill, and other industries and enterprises too numerous to mention." To Betts, however, these businesses alone "suffice to show the thrift and the stability of the commercial development of Huntsville." Further evidence of the growing urbanity of the town was demonstrated by the establishment of the Huntsville Gas Light Company in 1856 with a capitalization of $7,325.[67]

Unfortunately for Huntsville, its importance to the region made it a target of Union forces during the Civil War. Ironically, many Huntsville residents were opposed to immediate secession, and others remained so-called Unionists. With the advent of the war, however, Union forces were particularly attracted to Huntsville because of the presence of the

Memphis and Charleston Railroad, as well as the Madison Ironworks, which manufactured munitions for the Confederate army.[68] Unlike most cities in Alabama, which were left untouched during the war, Huntsville underwent several occupations by Union forces. The first such seizure occurred on April 11, 1862, when federal troops under the command of General Ormsby M. Mitchel took possession of Huntsville, without firing a shot, as his forces caught the town's sleeping citizens by surprise. In a letter to U.S. secretary of war Edwin M. Stanton dated April 17, 1862, General Mitchel reported that "on Friday, the 11th, I entered Huntsville, capturing a large number of engines and cars. On Saturday expeditions were dispatched by rail east and west, seizing Stevenson and Decatur. Decatur was at once occupied." Thus, the Confederacy's strategic east–west rail line of the Memphis and Charleston Railroad was severed. As for the Madison Iron Works, the Confederate forces had managed to remove the munitions-making machinery prior to the invasion of the Union forces. An entry into a journal kept by Huntsville resident Mary Jane Chadick during the Civil War described the occupation: "Truly our town is full of the enemy. There is a sentinel at every corner…They have been searching the houses today for arms." Although houses were searched as described, the Union

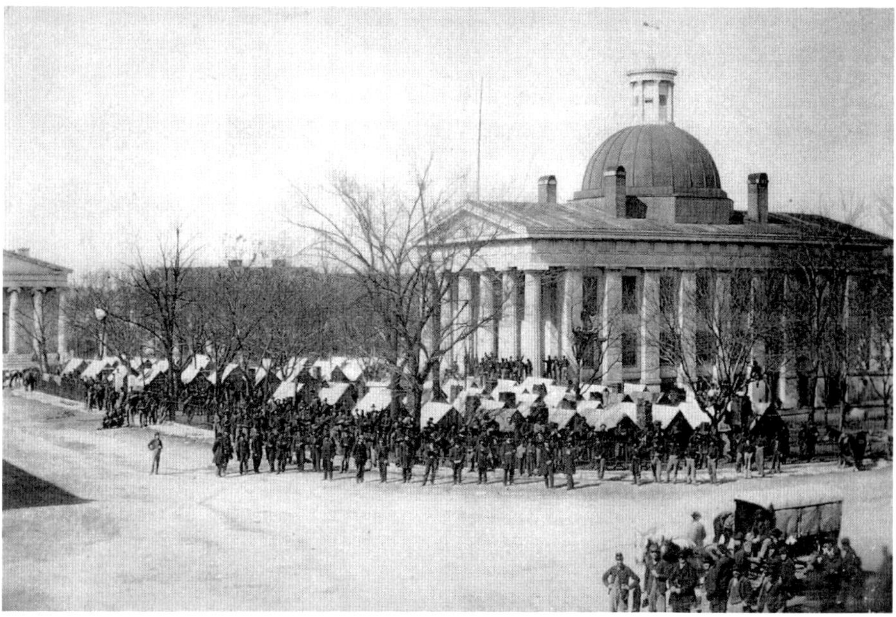

Federal soldiers occupying Huntsville's Courthouse Square in 1864. *Courtesy of Huntsville–Madison County Public Library.*

forces refrained from massive burning of residences or other buildings. A member of the Third Division Army of the Ohio wrote, "Huntsville is one of the most beautiful towns in America. There is a great deal of wealth here, the private residences are very elegant and surrounded with fine gardens. The air is so laden with perfume they call it Happy Valley." But he then added, "Alas it is no Happy Valley now."[69]

General Mitchel's occupation lasted until August 1862, when Mitchel was sent to South Carolina to take on a new command. Unfortunately for the citizens of Huntsville, Federal forces returned on at least two other occasions, using the town as an off-and-on base of operations in the Tennessee Valley for the remainder of the war. When the war finally did end, Huntsville suffered through Reconstruction like the rest of the state. Its economy was at first centered on the fruits of the area's fertile farmlands and the emergence of small cotton gins and mills. As Reconstruction came to an end, in the 1880s, Huntsville's economy expanded with the establishment of the Huntsville Cotton Mill, a telephone exchange, electric and gaslights and a rail line connecting the city to Nashville. In the 1890s, northern investors established commercial nurseries, which, along with fruit orchards and watercress farms, provided prosperous supplements to the continued production of cotton. Between the turn of the century and the Great Depression, Huntsville's economy grew and flourished. Its economy obviously suffered with the commencement of the Depression, but to worsen matters, it also suffered from a series of labor strikes in the textile industry. In 1933, however, Huntsville's recovery was boosted by the creation of the Tennessee Valley Authority, which brought the area jobs, enhanced flood control, improved river transportation and hydroelectric power.[70]

The onset of World War II brought dramatic changes to the economy of Huntsville when the federal government established the U.S. Army missile research program at the Redstone Ordnance Plant in 1941 on forty thousand acres of former cotton land and backwater a few miles south of the Tennessee River. In 1949, it was merged with the Huntsville Arsenal, which was a chemical warfare plant, to form the U.S. Army's new Ordnance Guided Missile Center. The next year, more than one hundred German scientists, led by rocketry pioneer Wernher von Braun, were transferred to this center to continue rocket and guided-missile research and development for the army. Huntsville and the von Braun team were put at the forefront of the federal government's commitment to put a man on the moon with the opening of NASA's Marshall Space Flight Center on July 1, 1960. At this center, von Braun's team developed and produced many components of

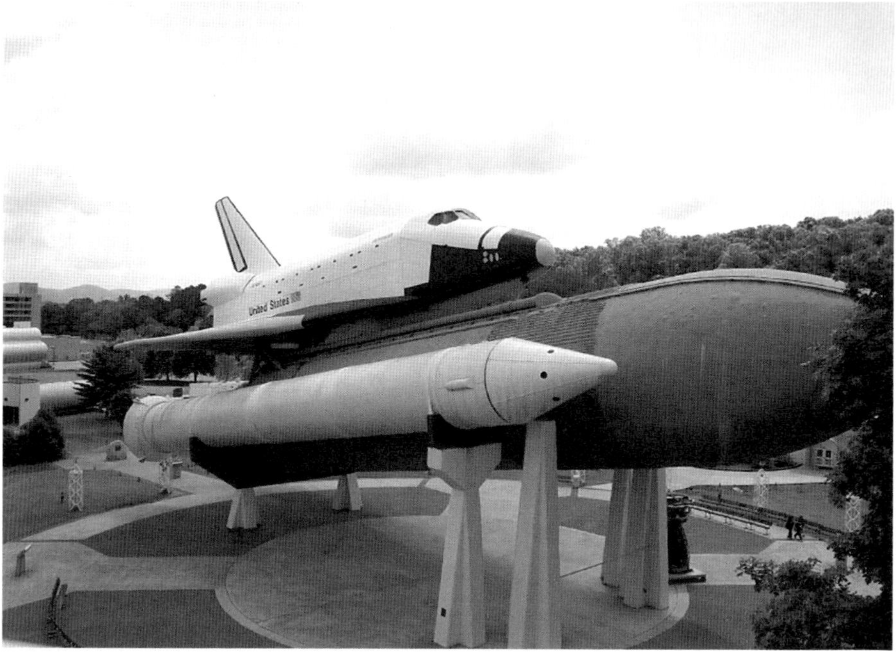

The U.S. Space and Rocket Center is reflective of Huntsville's prominent role in the U.S. space program. *Library of Congress.*

the Saturn V rocket, which would power men to the moon for the first time in history. After the last of the manned Apollo missions in the early 1970s, the Marshall Space Flight Center survived by turning its attention to the space shuttle, the International Space Station and emerging U.S. military technologies. Technology, space and defense industries still have a major presence in Huntsville with the army's Redstone Arsenal, NASA's Marshall Space Flight Center and Cummings Research Park. Home to several Fortune 500 companies, Huntsville also offers a broad base of manufacturing, retail and service industries. In 2010, Huntsville's population was 180,105, and the Huntsville Metropolitan Area's population was 417,593, making Huntsville the fourth-largest city in Alabama.[71]

Huntsville came a long way from John Hunt's founding of Big Springs in the early 1800s to the arrival of a group of German engineers led by Wernher von Braun, who enabled America to win the race with Russia to land a man on the moon. Today, tourists can stroll through the Constitution Village, a collection of reconstructed historic buildings, to see where Alabama's constitution came to fruition in a former cabinet

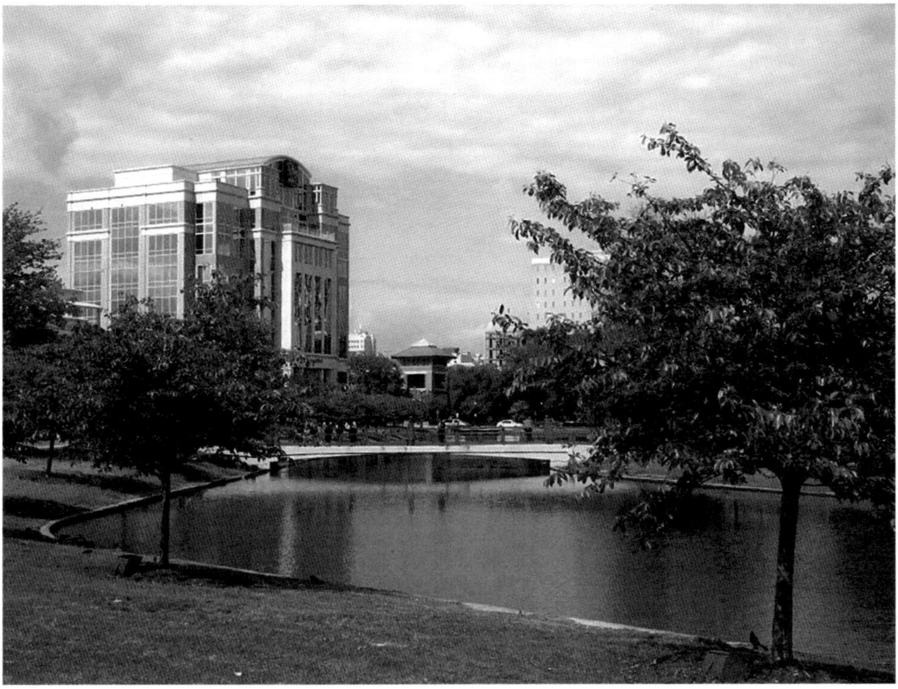

Photograph of the center of contemporary Huntsville looking toward Big Spring Park, where John Hunt first discovered Big Spring in 1805. *Library of Congress.*

shop. In addition, they can visit John Boardman's print shop, Clement Comer Clay's law office, the federal land surveyor's office, a post office and Sheriff Stephen Neal's residence. A few miles away from downtown Huntsville, they can also visit the U.S. Space and Rocket Center, recognized as one of the most comprehensive U.S. manned space flight hardware museums in the world. While Huntsville's reign as capital of the new state was short-lived, what was accomplished in such a short time was indeed amazing. Within approximately six months, a president was welcomed, a constitution crafted and a state government created. After the capital moved to Cahaba, Huntsville, unlike St. Stephens, was able to survive and flourish as a commercial, social, educational and cultural center, surrounded by the fertile lands of the Tennessee Valley. After surviving occupation during the Civil War, Reconstruction and the Great Depression, Huntsville is now one of Alabama's most vibrant cities.[72]

Chapter 3

Old Cahawba

Capital of Alabama (1820–1825)

History of the Site of Old Cahawba

For four thousand years, Native Americans had been living at the site of "Old Cahawba" (now Cahaba), which became Alabama's third capital in 1819. For the most part, the Indians who lived there were of the mound-building culture of the Mississippian period (AD 1000 to AD 1550). They migrated from the Gulf Coast to the banks of the Alabama River near where the Cahaba River flows into it and constructed a town a few miles southwest of present-day Selma, Alabama. This fortified town featured a moat, a palisade and a ceremonial or religious mound. Mound building was fairly widespread during this period, particularly in the fertile river valleys. Within this culture, large earthen mounds were thought to have served as monuments to the dead, homes of the leaders or as religious temples. Cahaba's mound builders are believed to have close cultural ties to the inhabitants of Bottle Creek, which is a significant archaeological site situated approximately twenty miles north of Mobile Bay.[73]

By the time the Spaniards, under Hernando de Soto, arrived in what was to become Alabama, the Mississippian culture was on the decline. There was, however, still a large Indian village at the site of Cahaba. To date, however, no concrete evidence has surfaced confirming that de Soto's conquistadores visited this site. Whether or not they visited this particular site, the overall indigenous Indian population had been exposed to these Europeans and the diseases they brought with them. Indeed, as much as

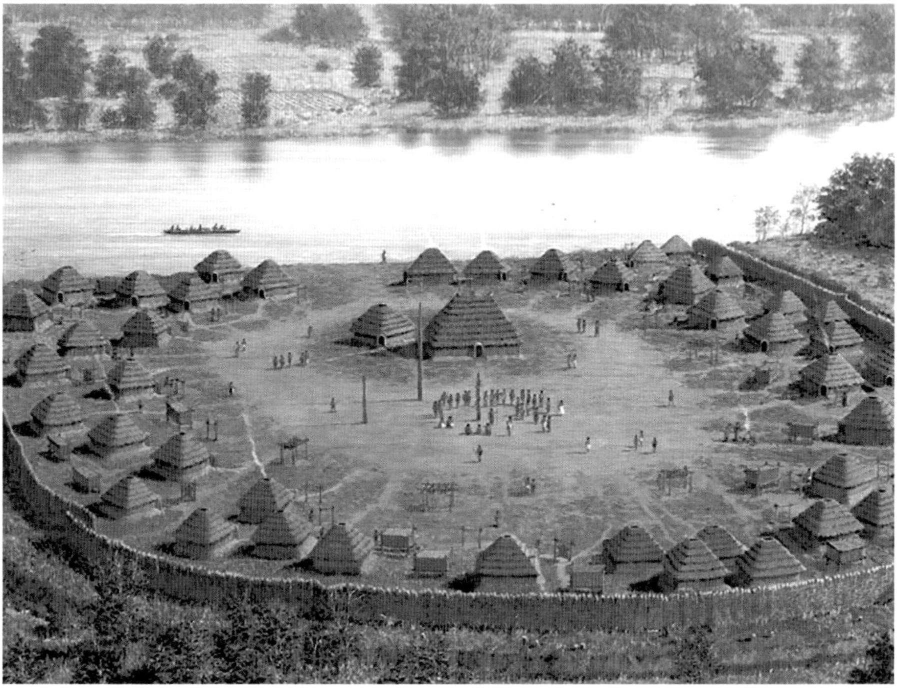

Painting of an ancient Native American village similar to the one that occupied the future site of Cahaba. *Courtesy National Park Service, painting by Lloyd Kenneth Townsend.*

50 percent of the native population was eradicated due to its exposure to smallpox, measles and other diseases. By the eighteenth century, most of the former Mississippian tribes had either vanished or were absorbed by the emerging cultures of the Creeks, Choctaws, Chickasaws and Cherokees. As a matter of fact, it is believed that a Choctaw town of considerable size existed at the site in the early eighteenth century but was abandoned well before Alabama became a territory. The name "Cahawba" is thought to have come from either two Choctaw words meaning "water above" or the Creek Indian word for the native cane that covered the river valleys. The "w" was dropped from the spelling in 1850, and the town was hence referred to as Cahaba. Both versions of the town's spelling will be utilized herein.[74]

The site of the confluence of the Alabama and the Cahaba Rivers was controlled at various times by France, Great Britain and Spain. It came under American control for the first time when it was ceded by Spain to the United States in 1795 in accordance with the Treaty of San Larenzo. At this time, the Cahaba River served as the Choctaws' eastern boundary with the Creek

Nation. With the defeat of the Creeks at Horseshoe Bend in 1814 and the resulting Treaty of Fort Jackson, millions of acres of Creek lands in central Alabama were opened up for settlement. The influx of settlers to this area was so great that it was called "Alabama fever." It was soon after Alabama became a territory in 1817 that its governor, William Wyatt Bibb, began to maneuver to have the state's "permanent" capital located at Cahaba.[75]

As we have seen, Governor Bibb had used his connections in Washington to secure passage of a bill that granted a free section of land for use as the state's seat of government and gave the governor the prerogative to select the site. While Tuscaloosa was the choice of a commission that had been appointed by the legislature to recommend the capital's location, Governor Bibb attached a rider to an apportionment bill favorable to north Alabama that provided for Cahaba to become the state's capital. To further placate northern representatives, Huntsville was selected as the temporary capital until Cahaba was made ready to serve as the state's permanent capital. In November 1818, Governor Bibb sought to justify his decision to choose Cahaba as the site for the state's first capital and outlined his great vision for that site:

> *I proceeded to examine the junction of Cahawba and Alabama. The bluff on the west side of those rivers, presents a beautiful site, with springs of good water, and the prospect of health. Situated on a river capable of being navigated by boats of great burthen, and supported as it will be, by the abundant productions of an extensive land for the back country on the Alabama and Cahawba, and their tributary streams, the town of Cahawba promises to vie with the largest inland towns in the southern country.*[76]

Having won the day in securing Cahaba as the capital of the new state, the General Assembly appointed Bibb as "commissioner with full power to lay off, or cause to be laid off on such plan as he may deem most suitable, a town at the place now called and known as the town of Cahawba." The assembly then gave Governor Bibb the task of surveying the lots and selling them to the highest bidders after having given notice of at least ninety days to prospective buyers through advertisements in all of the newspapers within the territory, as well as in newspapers in other states as deemed appropriate by him. Bibb was further given the authority to take the proceeds from the sale of these lots, in an amount not to exceed $10,000, to contract for the construction of "a building suitable for the temporary accommodation of the General Assembly of the territory or the [anticipated] state." With so

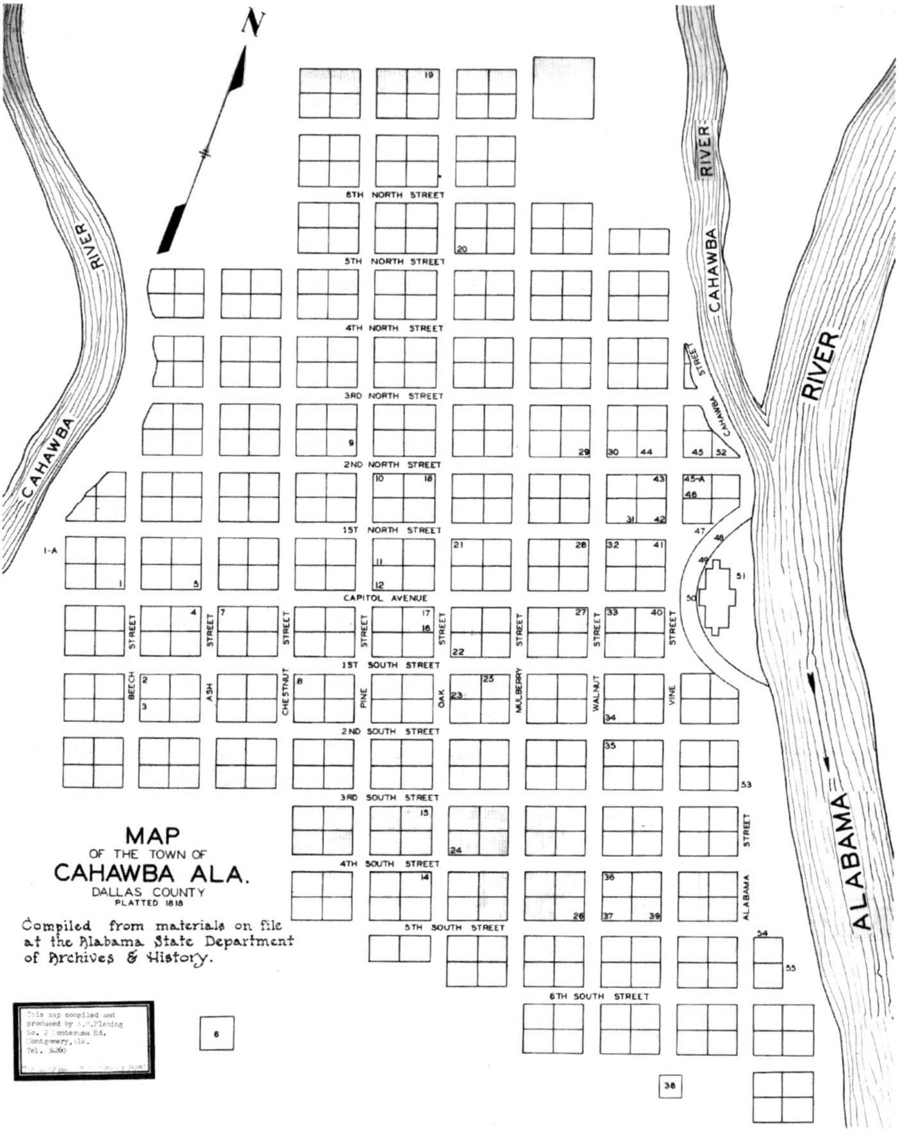

A map depicting the layout of old Cahaba. *Courtesy Alabama Department of Archives and History.*

little money made available for the construction of a capitol, forces were already trying to make sure that Cahawba would be only a temporary seat of government.[77]

Highest bidders for these lands were to pay one-fourth of the purchase money in hand, for which they were to receive a certificate from the governor, specifying the lot purchased by its number, its sales price and the amount paid. Purchasers could pay installments of one-fourth down, one-fourth within a year, one-fourth within two years and one-fourth within three years. Sales were so brisk that the federal land office was moved from Milledgeville, Georgia, to Cahawba about the time that Cahawba's town lots were opened for sale. To take advantage of the brisk sales, Governor Bibb was successful in increasing the original federal land grant for the state capital from 620 acres to 1,620 acres. Governor Bibb, who personally attended the auctions, reported that in May 1819, 182 lots had been sold for a total of $123,856, with 2 of the choicest lots going for approximately $5,000 each. Many of Alabama's early leaders purchased lots, including Reuben Saffold, Uriah J. Mitchell, Samuel Dale, Jesse Beene, William Rufus King, John Crowell, Thomas Bibb, Israel Pickens, Gabriel Moore, Clement C. Clay and Henry Hitchcock. An early settler of the area observed of these auction sales, "It was a perfect harvest for the tavern keepers, merchants, and liquor sellers" because as soon as the settlers in the surrounding area heard that the new capital was to be located in Cahawba, they "poured in like bees setting on a limb where they could find the queen had pitched her quarters."[78]

Governor Bibb's extravagant visions for the future of Alabama's capital in the wilderness were manifested in the way in which he laid out the town that was purportedly modeled after the nation's former capital of Philadelphia. Indeed, its streets bore some of the same names as those of the City of Brotherly Love, including Walnut, Oak, Mulberry, Chestnut, Ash, Peach and Pine. Capitol Avenue, which was one hundred feet wide and ran from the capitol westward to the Cahaba River, was the new town's central thoroughfare. All the other streets were just eighty feet wide, with the east–west streets numbered while the north–south streets were named for trees, as noted above. Each block on these streets contained four lots that all comprised one-half acre. Even before opening town lots for sale, Governor Bibb placed a notice in St. Stephens's *Halcyon and Tombeckbe Public Advertiser* on April 5, 1819, eagerly inviting bids for the construction of Alabama's first capitol building. In this invitation for bids, the governor gave very detailed specifications:

> *The building to be two story, fifty-eight feet long, and forty-three feet wide; each story to be twelve feet in the clear. The interior to be divided above and below stairs by a passage fourteen feet wide, on one side of which shall be one room the whole width of the house, and on the other, two rooms. Two chimneys and eight windows are to be provided at each end and twelve*

> *windows on each front of the building; each window to be twenty-four lights, 8 x 10...The shingles are to be of cypress or heart pine.*[79]

Agreeing to these specifications, David and Nicholas Crocheron of Dallas County were awarded the contract to build Alabama's first statehouse for the sum of $9,000. Governor Bibb reported to the General Assembly in Huntsville on October 26, 1819, that "[t]he principle parts of the building are to be finished on or before the first day of August next [1820]." It is not known precisely when construction began on the capitol, but it is clear that work was underway when the state's first General Assembly met in Huntsville in October 1819 because Governor Bibb reported to the assembly, "I learn that the building has been commenced, and that no doubt is entertained of its completion within the time specified in the contract." With the completion of construction, offices for the governor and the executive branch were made available on the first floor, while separate chambers for the House and the senate were located in two large rooms on the second floor. The completed structure was capped off with a shiny copper dome and was ready to house the state's government.[80]

Alabama's First State Capital (1820–1825)

Even prior to the completion of the statehouse and the convening of the state's first General Assembly, state government commenced in Cahawba on the second Monday of May 1819, when members of the judicial branch met there to organize Alabama's first Supreme Court and to convene its first session. Due to the absence of public buildings, Alabama's first justices—Abner S. Lipscomb, Reuben Saffold, Henry Y. Webb, Richard Ellis and Clement Comer Clay—convened in the private home of William Pye, who was compensated twenty dollars for the use of his house "and other accommodations." After adopting its rules of procedure and choosing Clement Comer Clay to serve as chief justice, the court proceeded to issue nine published decisions. These decisions were all of a civil nature and served as the origin of Alabama's precedential case law. Although most of these decisions involved technical issues relating to such matters as venue and pleading, there was one interesting decision that dealt with Alabama's colonial past. In that case, the court held that prior citizens of the Spanish-held territory of Louisiana were not competent to serve as jurors in Alabama unless they could prove that they were either naturalized U.S. citizens or citizens of Louisiana at the time Louisiana became a state in 1812.[81]

Not long after the Supreme Court completed its inaugural sessions, and while the frontier settlers were eagerly awaiting the arrival of the remainder of the state's government to their town, all Alabamians were shocked with the news of the death of Governor Bibb, who passed away on July 10, 1820. Not in robust health, Bibb's condition increasingly worsened due to injuries sustained when he fell from his horse while riding on his plantation near Coosada in Autauga County. Governor Bibb, only thirty-nine at the time of his death, was survived by his wife, two children and a brother, Thomas. Because Thomas Bibb was the president of the senate, he succeeded his brother as governor in accordance with the Constitution of 1819. Regrettably, William Wyatt Bibb did not live to see the completion of the capitol building that he fought so hard to locate in Cahawba, and his untimely death left Cahawba without its principal sponsor. In an obituary notice, Attorney General Henry Hitchcock eulogized Governor Bibb in part: "In the discharge of his domestic duties he was zealous, constant, and parental; he did not praise virtue without practicing it, and he was incapable of professing an excellence which he did not possess." Hitchcock continued, "Amidst all the vicissitudes of party, and the violence of faction, incident to a republic, and in which he held for many years a conspicuous station, his enemies never contradicted the character given him by his friends." Members of the General Assembly wore black crepe on their left arms for the remainder of their first session and passed an act changing the name of Cahawba County to Bibb County in honor of the late governor.[82]

When the General Assembly met in Cahawba for the first time on November 6, 1820, Governor Thomas Bibb lamented to its members that he had assumed the office of governor "with the most peculiar sensations of pain…rising not only from the reflection of the loss of a more experienced officer than myself, but also from a recollection which is continually renewed, that of the loss of a friend and a brother." Appropriately, one of the first issues addressed by the acting governor was the completion of the statehouse, which had begun and had been supervised by his brother. In this regard, Thomas Bibb reported to the assembly that the capitol building was almost complete, but not within the time specified by the contract with the Crocheron brothers. However, since the delay was deemed caused by unforeseen circumstances, and since the assembly was in immediate need of a place to convene, Governor Bibb recommended that they go ahead and accept the building with the proviso that it be completed as soon as

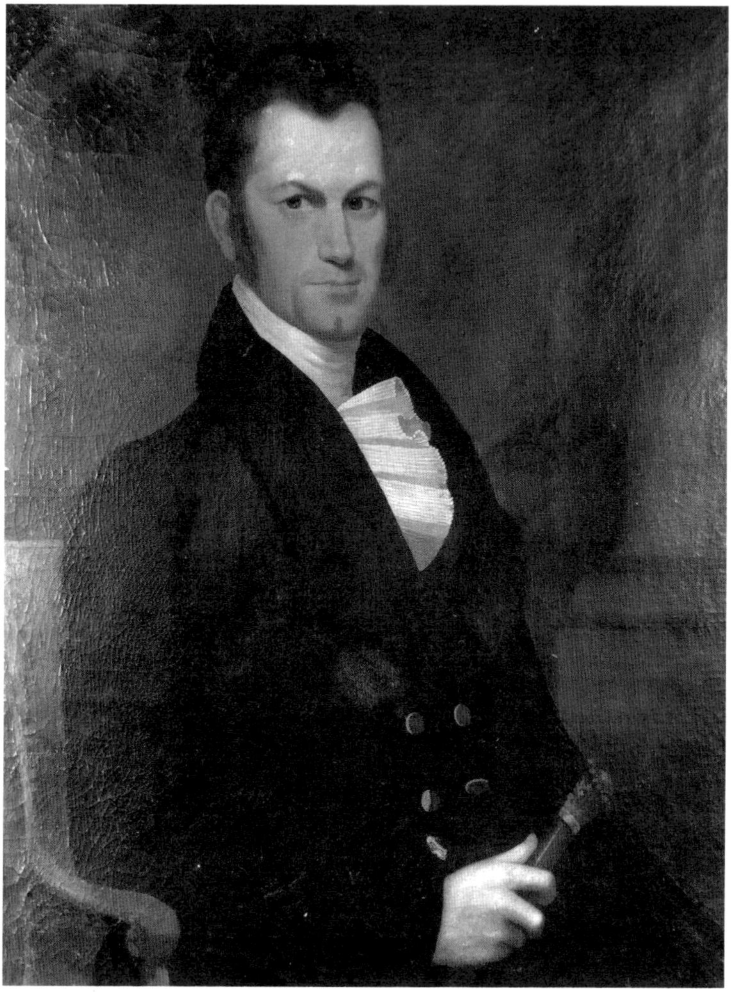

Governor Thomas Bibb (1783–1839), Alabama's second governor and brother of William Wyatt Bibb, Alabama's first governor. *Courtesy Alabama Department of Archives and History.*

possible thereafter. The Crocherons, however, sought an additional $4,500 due to extra work being performed under difficult circumstances. After an extensive debate, the assembly agreed to their request, driving the total cost to $13,500, not including $616 expended for furnishings for the capitol.[83]

When the various state officials arrived in Cahawba in November 1820, the town had not been entirely completed, but it was well on its way to becoming the state's seat of government, as well as its business, social and cultural center. In anticipation of the needs these officials, several inns, taverns and boardinghouses were already open for business when they arrived. That these establishments eagerly sought the business of the incoming legislators is evidenced by an advertisement appearing on September 29, 1820, in one of the local newspapers for the Arch Street Hotel, which was located across the street from the statehouse. This ad emphasized that the owner's "utmost exertions will be used to render their customers comfortable by endowing their tables with the finest foods available, keeping their rooms clean and stocking their bars with genuine liquors." The ad further stressed

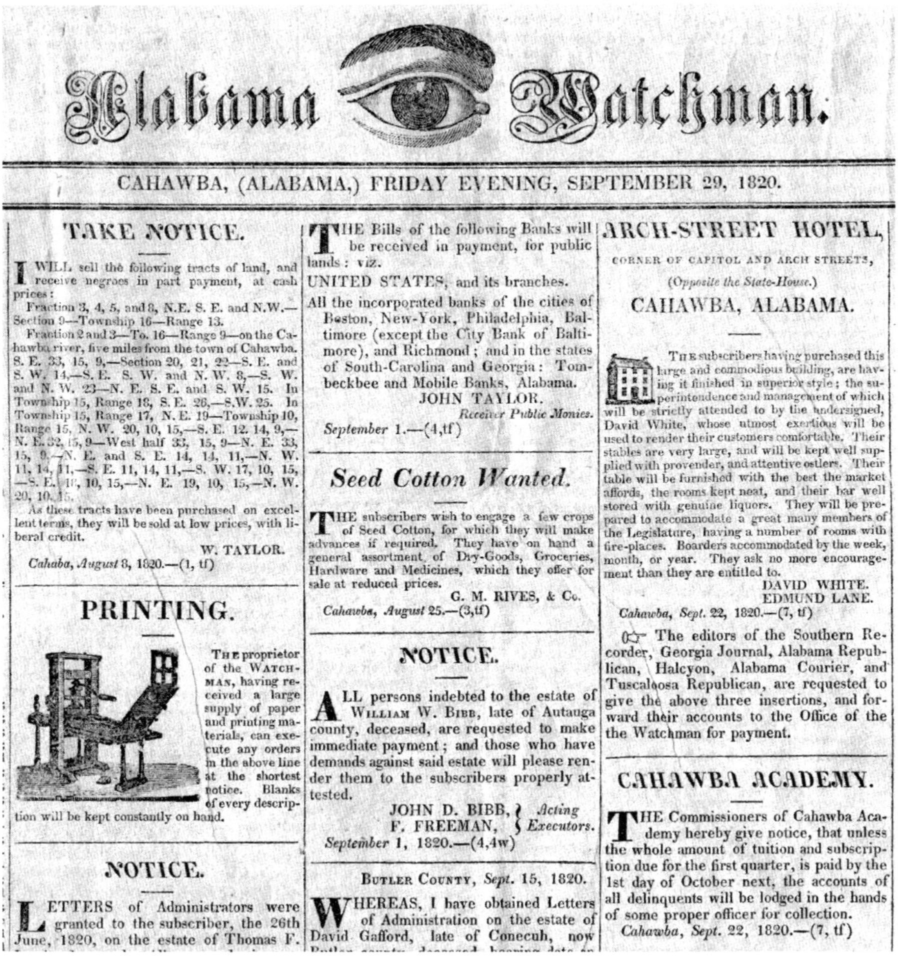

Alabama Watchman.

CAHAWBA, (ALABAMA,) FRIDAY EVENING, SEPTEMBER 29, 1820.

TAKE NOTICE.

I WILL sell the following tracts of land, and receive negroes in part payment, at cash prices:

Fraction 3, 4, 5, and 8, N.E. S. E. and N.W.—Section 9—Township 16—Range 13.

Fraction 2 and 3—To. 16—Range 9—on the Cahawba river, five miles from the town of Cahawba. S. E. 33, 15, 9,—Section 20, 21, 22—S. E. and S. W. 14,—S. E. S. W. and N. W. 8,—S. W. and N. W. 23—N. E. S. E. and S. W. 15. In Township 15, Range 18, S. E. 26,—S.W. 25. In Township 15, Range 17, N. E. 19—Township 10, Range 15, N. W. 20, 10, 15,—S. E. 12. 14, 9,—N. E. 32, 15, 9—West half 33, 15, 9—N. E. 33, 15, 9,—N. E. and S. E. 14, 14, 11,—N. W. 11, 14, 11,—S. E. 11, 14, 11,—S. W. 17, 10, 15,—S. E. 18, 10, 15,—N. E. 19, 10, 15,—N. W. 20, 10, 15.

As these tracts have been purchased on excellent terms, they will be sold at low prices, with liberal credit.

W. TAYLOR.

Cahaba, August 8, 1820.—(1, tf)

PRINTING.

THE proprietor of the WATCHMAN, having received a large supply of paper and printing materials, can execute any orders in the above line at the shortest notice. Blanks of every description will be kept constantly on hand.

NOTICE.

LETTERS of Administrators were granted to the subscriber, the 26th June, 1820, on the estate of Thomas F.

THE Bills of the following Banks will be received in payment, for public lands: viz.

UNITED STATES, and its branches.

All the incorporated banks of the cities of Boston, New-York, Philadelphia, Baltimore (except the City Bank of Baltimore), and Richmond; and in the states of South-Carolina and Georgia: Tombeckbee and Mobile Banks, Alabama.

JOHN TAYLOR.

Receiver Public Monies.

September 1.—(4,tf)

Seed Cotton Wanted.

THE subscribers wish to engage a few crops of Seed Cotton, for which they will make advances if required. They have on hand a general assortment of Dry-Goods, Groceries, Hardware and Medicines, which they offer for sale at reduced prices.

G. M. RIVES, & Co.

Cahawba, August 25.—(3,tf)

NOTICE.

ALL persons indebted to the estate of WILLIAM W. BIBB, late of Autauga county, deceased, are requested to make immediate payment; and those who have demands against said estate will please render them to the subscribers properly attested.

JOHN D. BIBB, } *Acting*
F. FREEMAN, } *Executors.*

September 1, 1820.—(4,4w)

BUTLER COUNTY, *Sept.* 15, 1820.

WHEREAS, I have obtained Letters of Administration on the estate of David Gafford, late of Conecuh, now

ARCH-STREET HOTEL,

CORNER OF CAPITOL AND ARCH STREETS,

(*Opposite the State-House.*)

CAHAWBA, ALABAMA.

THE subscribers having purchased this large and commodious building, are having it finished in superior style; the superintendence and management of which will be strictly attended to by the undersigned, David White, whose utmost exertions will be used to render their customers comfortable. Their stables are very large, and will be kept well supplied with provender, and attentive ostlers. Their table will be furnished with the best the market affords, the rooms kept neat, and their bar well stored with genuine liquors. They will be prepared to accommodate a great many members of the Legislature, having a number of rooms with fire-places. Boarders accommodated by the week, month, or year. They ask no more encouragement than they are entitled to.

DAVID WHITE.
EDMUND LANE.

Cahawba, Sept. 22, 1820.—(7, tf)

☞ The editors of the Southern Recorder, Georgia Journal, Alabama Republican, Halcyon, Alabama Courier, and Tuscaloosa Republican, are requested to give the above three insertions, and forward their accounts to the Office of the the Watchman for payment.

CAHAWBA ACADEMY.

THE Commissioners of Cahawba Academy hereby give notice, that unless the whole amount of tuition and subscription due for the first quarter, is paid by the 1st day of October next, the accounts of all delinquents will be lodged in the hands of some proper officer for collection.

Cahawba, Sept. 22, 1820.—(7, tf)

Alabama Watchman, September 29, 1820, one of Cahaba's two weekly newspapers. *Author's collection.*

that the owner was "prepared to accommodate a great many members of the Legislature, having a number of rooms with fireplaces," and that customers could be accommodated by the week, the month or the year. In addition to the hostelries accommodating the needs of the newly arriving citizens, access into Cahawba had been improved by ferries on the Cahaba and Alabama Rivers, and merchants were briskly building spacious stores to further meet the needs of the town's new citizens. Among the first mercantile establishments in Cahawba were John and Israel Crocheron Company, Henderson and Lowery and Company, Thos. H. Wiley and Co. and Trevis & McGimpsey. The Crocherons, located at North Second Street, advertised themselves as selling "Groceries, Dry-Goods, and Hardware, etc."[84]

In addition to inns and mercantile establishments, Cahawba also already had two weekly newspapers eager to appeal to its new citizens—the *Alabama Watchman* and the *Cahaba Press and Alabama State Intelligencer*. Artisans such as blacksmiths, carpenters, hostlers and hatters, in addition to the innkeepers and merchants, advertised their businesses in these two papers. By 1820, Cahawba also had attracted several physicians and lawyers to service the increasing population. Among the physicians were Drs. Casey and Lesly, who advertised in the *Alabama Watchman*: "Having entered into co-partnership in the practice of medicine, tender their services to the citizens of Cahawba and its vicinity, in the various branches of their profession. They have on hand a large assortment of fresh medicines, which they will dispose of on reasonable terms." Other physicians locating in Cahawba at this time were Dr. Thomas O. Meux and Dr. Edward Gantt. In 1823, Dr. Meux was elected by the Alabama General Assembly to serve on the Medical Board of Cahawba. Among the lawyers residing or practicing in Cahawba at this time were William Rufus King, Jesse Beene, Horatio G. Perry, Edwin Fay and Nathan Sargent. William Rufus King, who resided on a plantation between Cahawba and Selma, was elected as one of Alabama's first U.S. senators and later became vice president of the United States in 1853. Jesse Beene went on to serve on the Dallas County court and represented Dallas County in both houses of the Alabama General Assembly.[85]

The new capitol building, located in the center of the square on the corner of Vine Street and Capitol Avenue, was soon to become the center of activity of the town, which was quickly emerging from the surrounding wilderness. It was just across from Arch Street and was laid out on top of the ruins of a semicircular moat that had been built by Native Americans who had previously inhabited the site. Anna Gayle Fry, a subsequent resident of Cahaba, described the capitol as "a solid square brick structure, two stories

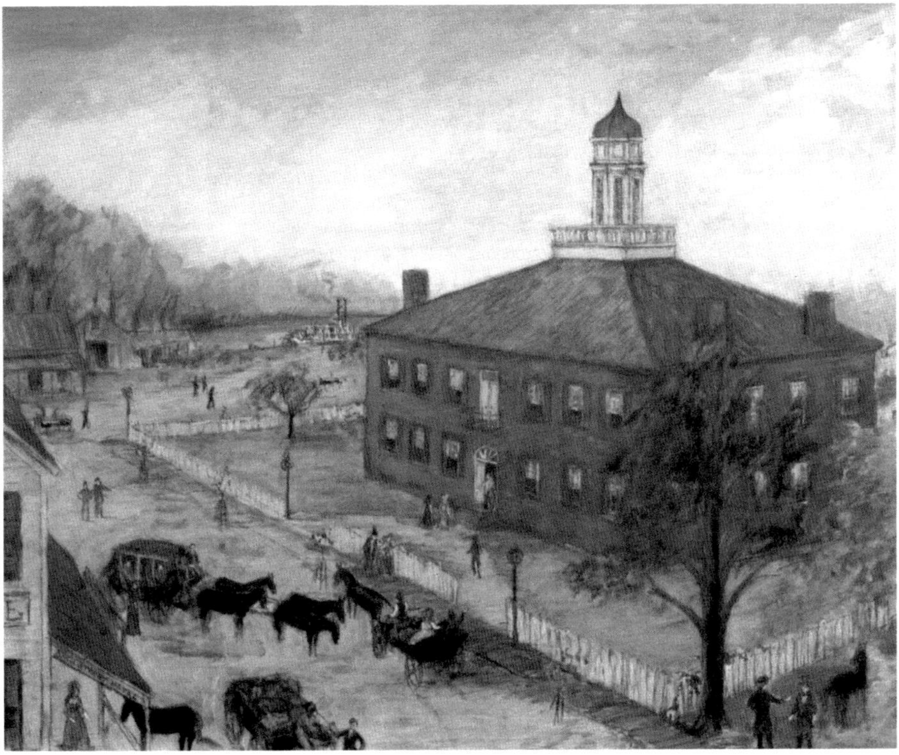

A contemporary painting depicting the capitol at Cahaba based on written reports of the period. *Courtesy of the artist, Dr. Robert O. Mellown, retired professor of art and architectural history, University of Alabama.*

high, surmounted by an imposing dome, said to be similar in appearance to the old capitol building of St. Augustine, Fla., which was erected in the same year." According to Fry, "Capitol Avenue was one of the fashionable residence streets that extend east and west through the center of town." As for Vine Street, she said it "was at that time and continued to be the principal business street of the town [and] was ornamented by ancient shade trees, gnarled and seamed; china berry, mulberry, and water oaks lined the streets on each side."[86]

Since there were no church buildings in the early days of Cahawba, the General Assembly allowed services to be held in the capitol building. An announcement of one such service appeared in the *Cahawba Gazette:* "Devine [*sic*] Services will be performed by the Rev. Mr. Herring in the State House, tomorrow, at the usual hour." Perhaps the earliest denomination to formally organize in Cahawba was the Alabama Presbytery, which convened there on

March 1, 1821. This was presumably the result of a Presbyterian missionary tour led by Reverend Thomas C. Stuart that had reached Cahawba in December 1819. Within a couple of years, the Alabama Bible Society convened its organizational meeting in Cahawba in 1823 and published its first annual report on December 16, 1824. For those living outside of Cahawba, in 1819, itinerant preachers had begun riding the circuit into the area to hold camp meetings for their benefit. On August 2, 1819, for example, a camp meeting was held on the Alabama River some thirty miles below Cahawba. Although the population was sparse and included many who were reportedly afflicted with a prevailing fever, at least "some were brought...to the knowledge of the truth." Thirty miles north of Cahawba, another camp meeting was held on August 10, 1819, on the Cahaba River, during which "[a] numerous concourse of people attended and much good was done," including thirty-seven conversions to God. The last two sessions of this meeting were held "in a forest, and the Indians were fishing in the river while we were preaching and praying."[87]

One of the acts passed in the first session of the Alabama General Assembly to convene in Cahawba authorized a lottery for the purpose of raising a sum not exceeding $20,000 for constructing and furnishing a Masonic Hall for the use and benefit of Cahawba's Halo Lodge. Located at the southwest corner of Vine and First North Street, the building was a pretentious addition to the town when it was completed. Members of the Halo Lodge met in Cahawba as early as December 30, 1820, in a temporary lodge room where festivities were held in which one of the brothers of the lodge addressed the assembled members "in a most interesting and pathetic manner, and...to the highest gratification of every person present." The brethren then proceeded to the Arch Street Hotel, where they were treated to "an elegant dinner...after which a number of very appropriate toasts and songs were given, and everything was conducted with decency and in order—The evening was spent with a large party of ladies." The new lodge was completed perhaps as early as June 11, 1821, as a convention of delegates from nine of the subordinate lodges in the state assembled in the "hall of the Halo Lodge No. 21 in the town of Cahawba" to draft a constitution and a code of bylaws for a Grand Lodge for the state of Alabama. Those representing Cahaba's Halo Lodge were T.A. Rodgers, Dr. Thomas O. Meux and William B. Allen.[88]

By 1821, as businesses expanded and state government took hold, the population of Cahawba was growing also. A Montgomery newspaper reported that in 1821, Cahawba had approximately one thousand people while at about the same time Montgomery's population was only about six hundred. It further maintained that only Huntsville surpassed Cahaba in population and facilities but that the only other cities in the state that were even near Cahaba in population and importance were Tuscaloosa, Montgomery, Claiborne and Florence. A factor contributing to Cahawba's continuing ascension was the arrival of the steamboat *Tensas* upriver from Mobile in May 1820. Although many have assumed that the *Harriet* was the first steamboat to arrive at Cahawba in October 1820, a bill of lading dated May 25, 1820, reveals that the master of the steamboat *Tensas* took aboard at Claiborne "3 chairs" that were to be transported to the port of Cahawba to be delivered "unto Sam'l Pickens." There is no doubt, however, that the most celebrated journey was that of the *Harriet*, which became the first steamboat to make it as far north as Montgomery on October 22, 1821. Impressively, the *Harriet* had made the trip from Mobile in just ten days, including three days with stops at Claiborne, Cahawba and Selma. Importantly, the *Harriet* made it safely back to Mobile and carried not only passengers but bales of cotton as well. With this feat, Cahawba had immediate access to markets in both Mobile and Montgomery. From Mobile, it had access to markets around the world. One local newspaper noted that "[i]t is for the interest of every citizen to encourage a regular

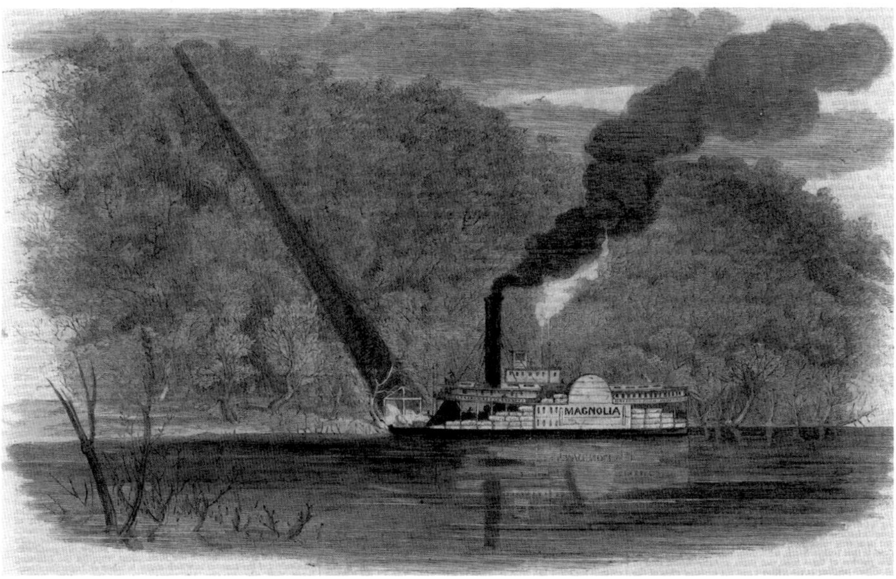

Sketch of a steamboat on the Alabama River. *Courtesy Alabama Department of Archives and History.*

line of Steam-Boats up the river." In time, the resourceful Crocheron family began to operate their own line of steamboats that ran from Cahawba to New York by way of Mobile and Cuba.[89]

Cahawba was bordered by the flowing waters of the Alabama and Cahaba Rivers on three sides and was susceptible to a fair amount of flooding. In the springs of 1821 and 1822, there had been heavy rains that caused the rivers to become swollen in "an unprecedented manner." In both of these years, there were additional heavy rains in July with resultant flooding. While the flooding was significant, it probably did not inundate the town to the extent that others would subsequently contend. The waters rose enough in each summer, however, to cause an outbreak of the deadly yellow fever. Cities such as Tuscaloosa and Montgomery had just the ammunition they wanted in their efforts to have the capital moved from Cahawba to their city. In the spring of 1822, when floodwaters isolated the capitol from the residential areas, a Montgomery newspaper exaggerated the situation by reporting that the legislators had to row up to second-story windows in order to get into the building. The *Montgomery Republican* additionally reported that "very few houses escaped the intrusion of the water; fifteen to twenty families were driven out of their homes by the water; the capitol was surrounded by water." On May 11, 1822, Cahaba's *Intelligencer* asserted that these claims were totally false and commented, "The able editor, whilst engaged in grinding the above, appears to have his head full of water." Although the Montgomery editor owned up to exaggerating his paper's reports of the flooding, it was too little, too late to repair the damage that had been done to the reputation of Cahawba.[90]

Amidst the background of political jockeying over the removal of the capital from Cahawba, the General Assembly continued to lay the foundation for the development of the new state. During the capital's tenure in Cahawba, eleven sessions of the Supreme Court were held, seven sessions of the General Assembly convened and four governors occupied office. As we have seen, after the death of Governor William Wyatt Bibb, his brother Thomas served as acting governor. During Thomas Bibb's short reign as governor, he urged a reapportionment of the legislature in accordance with the constitution. Oddly enough, the group favoring keeping the capital in Cahawba had grown to distrust their leaders' brother and successively delayed the consideration of the reapportionment issue during that session of the General Assembly. Thomas Bibb thus called the first special legislative session to meet in June 1821 to again urge the passage of reapportionment legislation, indicating that their failure to do so "threaten[ed] the very existence of the legislative branch of government." When a bill passed that exempted the senate from reapportionment until the first terms of senators would expire, Governor Bibb vetoed it. Thus, the main goal of Thomas Bibb's brief administration was not achieved, and Bibb decided not to seek reelection.[91]

Israel Pickens, a native of North Carolina and a former register of the land office in St. Stephens, became the third governor to serve in Cahawba after defeating Dr. Henry Chambers, a prominent physician from Huntsville. Pickens had distanced himself from the Georgia faction that he had originally supported when he quickly discovered that the so-called common folks considered it a party of the privileged few. Pickens, who had served as the president of the Tombeckbe Bank of St. Stephens, advocated the chartering of a state bank so as to transfer fiscal control away from the wealthy planter class, who, for the most part, controlled the private banks. The Planters and Merchants Bank of Huntsville, controlled by the Georgia faction, was particularly abhorrent to the common folks and yeoman farmers. Pickens's stance on the banking issue made him a "champion of the people" and catapulted him into the governor's chair.[92]

In his inaugural address delivered to a joint session of the Alabama General Assembly on November 9, 1821, Governor Pickens observed: "The fairest portion of our territory, and even the spot where we are assembled, was but yesterday unknown of the residence of civilized man. The prospects which nature alone presented have successfully invited a respectable order of emigration, and filled our forests with the improvements of good society." As Pickens settled into office, the main concerns of his administration were reapportionment and the establishment of a state bank. As for a state bank, the assembly passed a bill that would allow private banks to

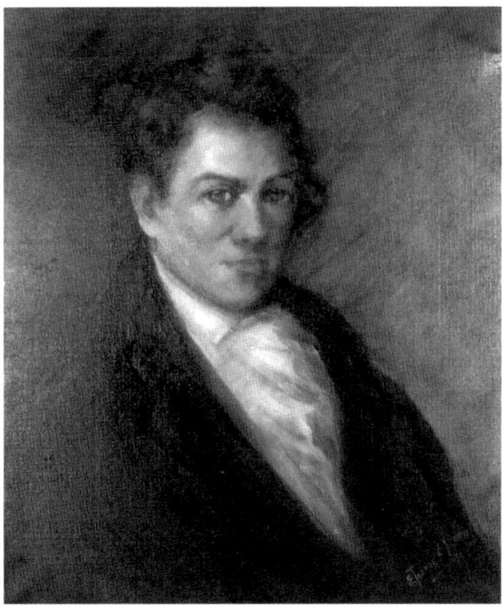

Governor Israel Pickens (1780–1827), third governor to serve in Cahaba. *Courtesy Alabama Department of Archives and History.*

become branches of the state bank and could actually maintain control over the state bank during its formative period. For this reason, and because he feared that the enormous debt of the private banks would be a burden on a fledgling state bank, Governor Pickens vetoed the bill and put the issue on hold until such time as he could get a bill with less influence allotted to the private banks. Meanwhile, the General Assembly was able to finally enact a reapportionment bill. All eyes of the competing capital relocation forces—i.e., the Tombigbee/Warrior group, which favored relocation to Tuscaloosa, and the Alabama/Cahaba group, which favored keeping the capital in Cahawba—were now focused on senatorial reapportionment since the relocation issue would be reconsidered by the General Assembly in 1825, and the vote would hinge on how many votes the competing groups picked up in the reapportionment.[93]

Governor Pickens was reelected in 1823, again defeating Dr. Henry Chambers of Huntsville by a comfortable margin. As soon as he took office in Cahawba for a second time, Pickens began to push hard for the establishment of a state bank now that both houses of the assembly were controlled by his supporters. The act called for an initial capitalization of a little more than $200,000. Approximately half of that amount was subscribed by the trustees of the University of Alabama in accordance with legislation enacted in the previous session of the assembly that authorized the board of trustees to invest in any bank to be created by the assembly in an amount not to exceed $100,000. The state bank opened its doors to the public in Cahawba in 1824, governed by a president and a board of directors to be elected on an annual basis by a combined vote of the General Assembly. The selection of bank officers and directors would be rank with a political odor, as evidenced by the fact that its first president was the governor's brother, Andrew Pickens, and that such prominent attorneys and politicians as Henry Hitchcock, Jesse Beene and Horatio G. Perry served on its first board of directors. The state bank would thereafter be embroiled in Alabama politics prior to its ultimate termination in the decade before the Civil War.[94]

As Governor Pickens's term as governor was coming to a close, and as the all-important reapportionment was soon to decide the outcome of the relocation of the seat of government issue, the citizens of Cahawba were teeming with excitement at the news that the Marquis de Lafayette, the aging French hero of the American Revolution, was going to stop in Cahaba during his triumphal tour of America in 1824–25, honoring the nation's fiftieth anniversary. Governor Pickens was given *carte blanche* by the Alabama General Assembly to roll out the red carpet for Lafayette and his entourage,

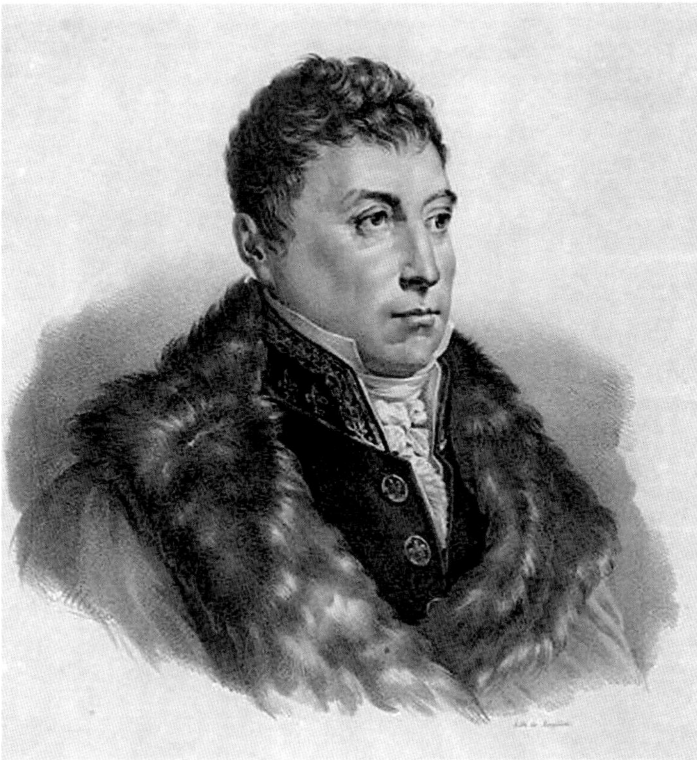

The Marquis de Lafayette (1757–1834), hero of the American Revolution, stopped in Cahaba during his triumphal tour of America in 1824–25. *Library of Congress.*

which consisted of his son, George Washington Lafayette; his secretary, Auguste Levasseur; and his dog, Quiz. Lafayette spent eight days in Alabama from March 31, 1825, when his entourage crossed the Chattahoochee River into Alabama near Fort Mitchell, until April 8, 1825, when he sailed from Mobile Point to New Orleans to continue his national tour. After a greeting by an Alabama delegation of officials and fifty Creek warriors led by Chilly McIntosh, Lafayette was treated to an intense game of ball play among the Creeks before he commenced his journey through the state.[95]

The first stop of importance on Lafayette's tour of Alabama was Montgomery, on April 3, 1825, where elegant speeches were delivered, extravagant receptions were conducted and a ball held in his honor. Governor Pickens had even arranged for a New Orleans orchestra to play for the Montgomery ball. Late in the evening of April 4, after the ball,

Lafayette and his entourage boarded the steamboat *Henderson* to continue their tour of Alabama. As the steamboat made its way downriver, a band played "patriotic airs" as onlookers on the riverbank cheered their hero and the most honored guest in the state's short history. At about nine o'clock on the morning of April 5, the *Henderson*, carrying Lafayette's entourage and two other steamboats carrying accompanying dignitaries, docked just long enough in Selma for some of its citizens to quickly come aboard the *Henderson* to greet Lafayette. After this brief stop, the group headed downriver for the short trip to Cahawba, where more lavish ceremonies awaited the legendary hero.[96]

Hundreds of Alabamians from as far away as Tuscaloosa greeted Lafayette when he reached the dock at Cahawba on the morning of April 5. Amid the sounds of canons booming, church bells ringing and the gathered crowd cheering, Lafayette was formally greeted by Governor Pickens as he stepped off the gangplank. As a band played "Lafayette's March," the governor escorted the honored guest up the river embankment that was lined by members of the Cahawba Guards, a company of local militia volunteers. As he reached the top of the bluff, Lafayette passed through a "large, beautiful triumphal arch," which, according to Anna Gayle Fry, had been constructed in his honor in the center of Vine Street, between Capitol Avenue and First North Street. Here he listened to a welcoming speech delivered by Alabama attorney general Henry Hitchcock, grandson of General Ethan Allen of Vermont, who had been a comrade in arms with Lafayette during the American Revolution. The party then proceeded to the statehouse, where, on the way, he reportedly passed through another arch where little girls preceded him, strewing flowers in his path. Two more receptions were held at the statehouse, where Lafayette was greeted by state officials and the leading men of the town upstairs in the House chamber and by the leading ladies of the town downstairs in the senate chamber.[97]

After the welcoming receptions, Lafayette was later fêted with a public barbecue, a formal dinner, a reception at the Masonic lodge and a ball. The barbecue was held outdoors at noon and was open to the general public, who could consume as much food and drink as they wanted. Anna Gayle Fry states in her memoir that "tradition has it" that the Bell Tavern, located on the corner of Vine Street and Second North Street, was the site of the "grand banquet" held for Lafayette. During this dinner, a series of thirteen toasts was given, to which the honored guest replied. After the dinner, Lafayette was taken to the Halo Lodge to intermingle with his fellow Masonic brethren before attending a ball in his honor. After the ball, Lafayette and his party once again boarded their steamboat to head down the river, with a short stop in Claiborne before arriving in Mobile, the last stop on his tour of Alabama.[98]

General Lafayette's secretary, Auguste Levasseur, reported his observations of the entourage's visit to Cahaba as follows:

> *It is difficult to imagine anything more romantic than the elevated, gravelly and, often times wooded shores of the Alabama...We stopped one day at Cahawba where the officers of the government of the State of Alabama, had in concert with the citizens, prepared entertainments for General Lafayette, as remarkable for their elegance and good taste, as touching by their cordiality and the feelings of which they were the expression. Among the guests with whom we sat down to dinner we found some countrymen whom political events had driven from France* [and who had settled in the Vine and Olive Colony in and around a small town they called "Demopolis."][99]

After Lafayette's departure from the capital, the *Cahawba Press* gave its readers an eloquent account of this historic visit:

> *What human sight could equal the appearance of Gen. Lafayette, when moving with slow and faltering step, he left the steamboat and landed on our river bank? Every eye of the immense multitude was strained to behold him, whilst the veteran patriotic pilgrim, with head uncovered, supported on the arm of the Governor, moved with slow and halting pace along the sandy acclivity of the bluff. He, who in the most dark and gloomy period of our revolutionary struggle repaired to our assistance, the great the good LAFAYETTE appeared among us, and every heart overflowed with love and gratitude, and greeted his reception.*[100]

As magnificent as this historic visit was, it was also a burden on the fledgling state's limited resources. When all was said and done, the state had expended approximately $20,000 on costs associated with Lafayette's visit. The grand sum of these expenses constituted about 20 percent of the state's budget for that year, payment of which pretty much depleted the funds in the state's treasury. When it is realized that only $10,000 was allotted for the construction of the capitol building in Cahawba and that no funds had yet to be expended on the construction of buildings for the University of Alabama, a total expenditure of $20,000 was indeed a burden on the state's limited resources. The expenses would have been even higher had not two of the escorting cavalry units covered their own expenses. In any event, the visit had been a grand success as Alabamians from all over the state traveled to witness in person the last living hero of the American Revolution and one of the world's most celebrated citizens.[101]

As the dust settled from Lafayette's visit, Alabama's leaders once again turned their attention to the relocation of the capital issue that was scheduled to be taken up in the upcoming 1825 session of the General Assembly. This issue heated back up just as Governor Pickens's term was coming to an end. Pickens's influence was such, however, that he was able to handpick John Murphy of Monroe County as his successor, who was elected without opposition. Since both Pickens and Murphy opposed the capital's relocation to Tuscaloosa, in his last address to the General Assembly, Governor Pickens proposed a plan to give the Alabama River region a chance at securing the capital if the assembly voted to move it from Cahawba. This plan called for requiring the next capital to be located at a new tract of land on which an entire metropolis could be laid out. This, of course, by definition would disqualify the existing town of Tuscaloosa, while at the same time allowing a new site to be selected within the Alabama River system not possessed of the problems of flooding and health issues as encountered in Cahawba. After much maneuvering, however, the Warrior/Tombigbee faction won the day when the assembly voted to relocate the capital to Tuscaloosa on December 13, 1825. Since Governor Murphy was without veto power with respect to this issue, Cahawba's reign as the seat of government would soon come to an end.[102]

The capital was on the road again to a new location. To facilitate the move to Tuscaloosa, the General Assembly passed legislation requiring the comptroller, treasurer and secretary of state "to adopt such measures for the removal of their respective offices…either by land or water conveyance, and also for the transportation of such furniture…as may be convenient." Legislation also required the senate doorkeeper to round up the furniture of each branch of government and store it in the senate chamber, which was to be locked and the key left in the possession of the state treasurer. The treasurer was given the authority to sell any furniture not taken to Tuscaloosa. He also had the authority to sell the statehouse itself provided it sold for at least $3,000.[103]

As summarized in *Clearing the Thickets: A History of Antebellum Alabama*, "The focus in Cahaba had been on organizing state government and providing for the basic needs of its citizens, particularly with regard to safety and security."

Indeed, Alabama's state government had been forged in Cahawba as a result of legislation enacted by the General Assembly between October 1819 and January 1826. During this period, more than eight hundred bills had been enacted into law, many of which helped to lay the foundation for the new state's government, such as those that "dealt with organizing the state government and its legal system; apportioning the legislature; organizing a state militia; creating towns and counties; raising revenue and imposing taxes; providing for internal improvements; providing funding for education by the sale of public lands; creating a state bank; and deciding upon an permanent seat of government."[104]

Temporary Resurrection after Capital's Relocation to Tuscaloosa

As the state government began the trek to its new home in Tuscaloosa, Cahawba immediately went into a decline, as evidenced by the number of abandoned homes and the exodus of many of its residents to places such as Mobile and Tuscaloosa. Soon the population was as low as three hundred, down from over one thousand. Although it remained the county seat of Dallas County, Cahawba soon took on the appearance of a ghost town. Anna Gayle Fry reported that not only were many of the houses torn down or abandoned but also "[r]are flowers bloomed in the lonely yards in neglected wild luxuriance" and "climbing roses waved mournfully to the breeze from decaying galleries, and the grass grew in the principal streets as though months had passed since foot had touched it." Cahawba continued to struggle during the early 1830s, when it was hit by another flood. In 1831, a visiting Englishman by the name of Thomas Hamilton was unimpressed with Cahawba, finding it to be "a very poor collection of very poor houses." In 1838, Phillip Henry Gosse, the famous naturalist from England who was teaching at Judge Reuben Saffold's plantation across the Alabama River from Cahawba, reported in his journal, *Letters from Alabama*: "Cahawba was formerly the seat of government of the state but it is now much decayed and has a very desolate appearance; a few 'stores,' a lawyer's office or two, and two or three tradesmen's shops." He concluded by stating that the busiest spots in town were the rum shops, which were teeming full of customers.[105]

Unlike St. Stephens, however, Cahawba was able to make a remarkable recovery, at least for a while, before the Civil War sent it into another decline from which it would not recover. Anna Gayle Fry described its recovery as a "Phoenix-like" rise from its ashes, allowing it to "again assume its old importance." Cahawba's resurrection was due to its location on the Alabama River in the midst of the rich soils of the Black Belt, where cotton was taking hold as the predominant crop. As a result, in the 1840s, Cahawba began to emerge as the shipping center for the area's cotton, which was sent down the Alabama River to Mobile, from whence it was shipped to the mills of New England and Great Britain. In the early 1850s, Cahaba was given another boost when it was learned that construction was forthcoming on a railroad to run between Cahaba and Marion in Perry County. The completion of the railroad in 1858 brought another boom to Cahaba, which by that time was populated by approximately two thousand people, the majority of whom were slaves who tended their owners' fields or worked in their shops.[106]

Cahaba prospered during the 1840s and 1850s as the nation headed inexorably toward war. During this period, many of its inhabitants were very prosperous and built elegant homes. Also, it was during this period that the original spelling of Cahawba was dropped in favor of the modern spelling, "Cahaba," for both the town and the river. Dallas County was the wealthiest in the state and ranked among the top five counties nationwide. Wealthy planters, with many slaves, ran plantations located in the surrounding countryside. John W. DuBose, early biographer of the fiery secessionist William Lowndes Yancey, who lived for a while in Cahaba, painted an idyllic picture of the former capital during this period: "In all America, in town or country, no people sat down to more bounteous dinners, served by better servants, on richer mahogany; no people wore more fashionable clothes rode better groomed horses, wrote a purer vernacular, or spoke it with gentler tones."[107]

Perhaps the most elegant house of the period was Perrine Mansion, built by Edward Martineau Perrine, who had relocated to Cahaba from New York. He was described by Anna Gayle Fry as "a merchant prince of the antebellum days, a Northern gentleman of the old school who was universally loved by all who knew him." This opulent twenty-six-room brick mansion, which had originally been built as a factory, was located at the foot of Vine Street. Its spacious grounds contained a conservatory, a greenhouse for grapes and an artesian well, believed at that time to be the deepest well in the world at approximately nine hundred feet. The house featured sweeping halls, parlors, reception rooms and even a ballroom. It was not unusual for its spacious dining room to accommodate up to one hundred guests seated around massive mahogany tables. Remarkably,

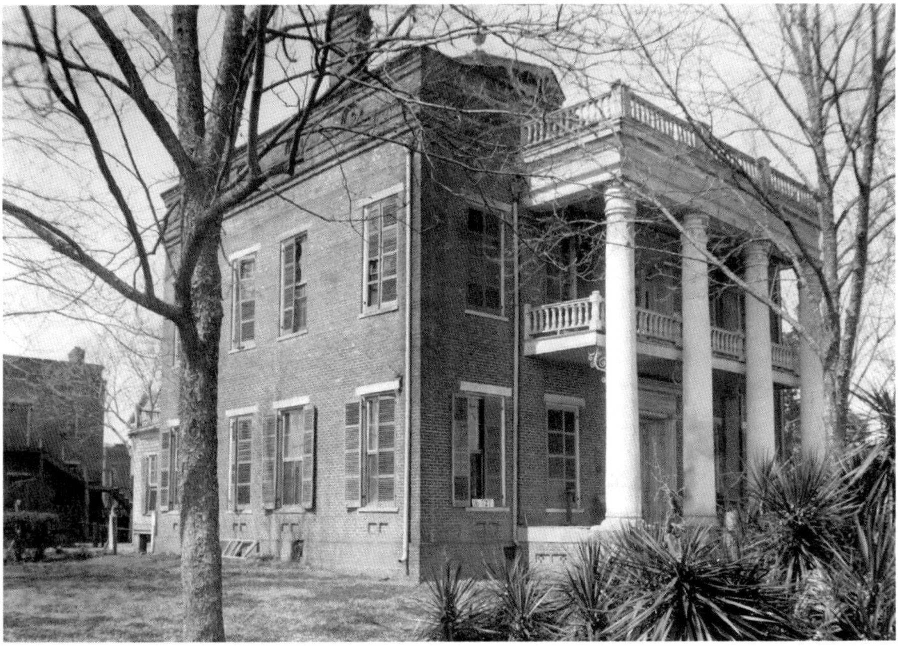

The Kirkpatrick Mansion on Oak Street is reflective of Cahaba's golden years. *Library of Congress.*.

the house was the first building in Alabama to have an air-conditioning system supported by abundant artesian waters pumped through pipes located throughout the house. Perhaps not as elegant as the Perrine Mansion but more symbolic for Cahaba was a house built about 1843 by Richard Conner Crocheron, who had migrated from New York to run a mercantile business. When his wife died in 1850, Crocheron sold his house, freed his slaves and returned to New York with his three children. Some of the round brick columns for this imposing edifice remain yet today. They are now referred to as the "Crocheron Columns" and have become a modern-day symbol of Old Cahaba.[108]

As further evidence of Cahaba's reemergence, Anna Gayle Fry noted "paved walks, large public buildings of bricks, [a] telegraph office, [an] insurance office, three well-edited papers, four churches, beautiful private residences, handsome suburban villas, and marvelous overflowing wells." Also of importance to rebounding Cahaba was the Cahaba Female Academy, which was in a large two-story, columned brick structure. It housed a library and a laboratory for philosophical and chemical research that reportedly cost several thousand dollars. Regarded at that time as one of the state's

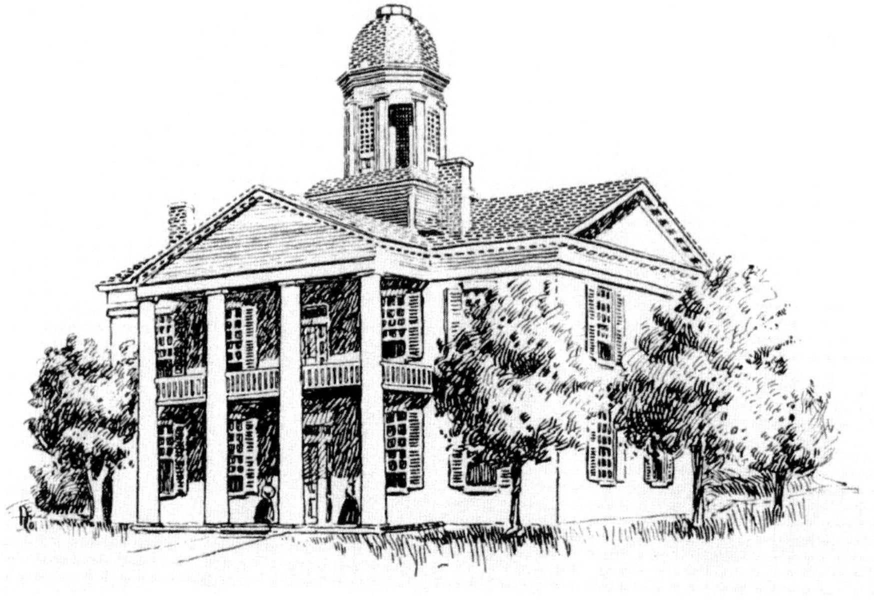

Sketch of the Cahaba Female Academy, which was regarded as one of the state's most important educational institutions for women at the time. *From* Memories of Cahaba.

most important educational institutions for women, it attracted students locally, as well as from other parts of the state. Advertised as the "second-finest in the state," Cahaba's principal hotel in the mid- to late 1850s was Dallas Hall. Located on the northwest corner of Vine and First North Street and a block south of Perrine's Store, it was remodeled in 1858 or 1859, and its name was changed to Aicardie's Hotel. These changes did not take away from its reputation for "magnificent cooking, elegant saloon, and fine bar." Saltmarsh Hall, located at the corner of Vine and First North Streets, was another impressive structure in Cahaba during its zenith. While part of the building was used as a Masonic lodge, the remainder of the building was a site for balls, parties and tableaux demonstrating historical, romantic and political scenes.[109]

The institution of slavery played a very prominent role in the history of Cahaba, as it provided the labor that enriched the planter class of Cahaba and Dallas County. By 1860, approximately 64 percent of Cahaba's population was African American, while in Dallas County as a whole, African Americans made up 75 percent of the population. African American slaves were sold at public sales in front of the county courthouse located on the first lot of First North Street up from Vine Street. Those slaves who lived or worked in

Cahaba were strictly controlled by a local ordinance. In this regard, every night at 9:00 p.m., a bell at the marketplace was rung as a warning to slaves to return to their homes. Any slave found on the streets without a pass from his or her owner was arrested by slave patrols. Called "patterollers or "patarollers" by the slaves, these patrols rode at night looking for runaway slaves or slaves off their plantations without passes. Those arrested in Cahaba were thrown into the local calaboose, located on the northwest corner of Walnut and Second North Streets next to the marketplace where the warning bell was sounded. There were at least a few free African Americans in Cahaba, two of whom—Sam Edwards and a person known as "Joe the Barber"—owned a barbershop in the block located at the corner of Second Street North and Vine Streets. Their former owners had freed them before leaving Cahaba and returning to the North. There were a few others who were able to purchase their freedom after becoming highly skilled craftsmen engaged in such crafts as bricklaying, carpentry, blacksmithing and plastering.[110]

Civil War and Reconstruction: The Final Death Knell for Cahaba

On the eve of the Civil War, Cahaba was at its pinnacle, with an estimated population of anywhere between three and six thousand. Unfortunately, however, the advent of the war ensured the eventual sounding of the death knell for Cahaba. Cahabians did not foresee the ruin that would overwhelm the region, and most of them enthusiastically supported the newly formed Confederacy. At the outset of the war, the local militia, known as the Cahaba Rifles, became attached to the Fifth Alabama Infantry Regiment as Company F, led by Captain Christopher C. Pegues. The company's flag was presented to the Cahaba Rifles at a ceremony conducted at Saltmarsh Hall, at which time Captain Pegues received the banner and vowed to carry it on to "victory or death." In early 1862, Captain Pegues was elected colonel of the Fifth Alabama Infantry Regiment. The Fifth Alabama was in turn attached to the Confederate Army of Northern Virginia and saw action in many significant battles, including Gaines Mill, Seven Pines, Malvern Hill, First Cold Harbor, Chancellorsville and Gettysburg. Colonel Pegues was mortally wounded at Gaines Mill on June 27, 1862, and died on July 15, 1862. Another Cahaba component to serve in the war was Lewis's Partisan Rangers, a cavalry unit that was organized by Thomas Lewis, a former lieutenant in the Cahaba Rifles. After growing rapidly to five companies, it became known as Lewis's Battalion and was attached to the Confederate Army of the Tennessee. It served at times under Nathan Bedford Forrest, John B. Hood and fellow Alabamian "Fighting Joe" Wheeler. Like Colonel Pegues, Major Lewis did not survive the war, losing his life during a skirmish in Lafayette, Georgia, in June 1864.[111]

A legendary ghost story pertaining to Old Cahaba featured Colonel Pegues, the leader of the Cahaba Rifles and the Fifth Alabama Infantry Regiment. The story commences with a young couple strolling the luxurious grounds behind Colonel Pegues's mansion in Cahaba on a moonlit night in the spring or summer of 1862. Their romantic stroll was suddenly interrupted when a ball of bright light appeared in front of them, swerving from side to side and getting close enough for them to attempt to touch but disappearing upon such attempts. After its disappearance, it would soon reappear again—but always escaping the reach of the young lovers. In one version of this story, it is speculated that the apparition could be the ghost of Colonel Pegues, who was mortally wounded at the Battle of Gaines Mill about the same time that the apparition was first seen by the young couple in the back of Colonel Pegues's mansion. In another version of the story, it was concluded that the apparition was

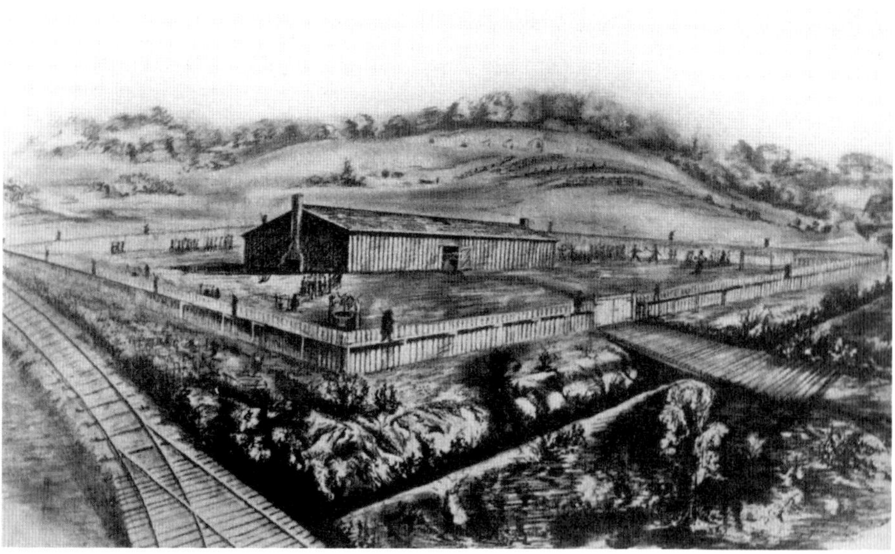

Sketch of "Castle Morgan," the local name for the Cahaba Federal Prison during the Civil War, which housed some three thousand prisoners of war. *Library of Congress.*

"one of those strange phosphorescent phenomena rarely seen, known as 'will-o-the-wisp' or 'Jack-o'-lantern.'"[112]

As the Civil War progressed, the Confederate government decided to confiscate the Cahaba-to-Marion railroad and used its rails and rolling stock instead to finish a more militarily significant line from Selma to Demopolis. Without the availability of Cahaba's railroad to bring it cotton, a warehouse under construction was left unfinished. The Confederate government decided to convert this unfinished structure, which overlooked the Alabama River, into a military prison for Federal prisoners of war. As part of the conversion of this facility into a prison, a large wooden stockade was built around it. The Cahaba Federal Prison, known locally as "Castle Morgan," opened in June 1863. Within five months, there were 660 Federal prisoners in this facility, which was designed to house only 500 prisoners. In August 1864, things got much worse when the Lincoln administration decided to end the customary practice of exchanging prisoners, causing the Confederate prisons to be overwhelmed with continuous new arrivals. With increasing numbers of prisoners arriving at the Cahaba Federal Prison, already difficult living conditions worsened. Unsanitary conditions, along with inadequate food, clothing, shelter and firewood, were bad enough for 500 or 600 prisoners but were greatly compounded by the presence of more than 3,000 prisoners by the end of the war. Despite these conditions, and although some prisoners died of pneumonia and dysentery, the prison death rate at Castle Morgan remained at less than 2 percent. This is astonishing considering the fact that the overall death rate in all Federal prisons was 12 percent and that in all other Confederate prisons, it was 15.5 percent. Many of the Federal prisoners at Castle Morgan were treated for their ailments alongside wounded Confederate soldiers at Bell Tavern, which had been converted into a military hospital. Unfortunately, as we shall soon see, many of the prisoners who survived their stay at Castle Morgan died in a tragic steamboat accident while they were being shipped to their homes back North.[113]

As the war wore on, Cahaba became a safe haven for civilian refugees from Union-occupied areas and areas of combat, so much so that in the last few months of the war, it is believed that Cahaba's population had mushroomed to approximately 6,000. On April 2, 1865, a few days before the surrender of General Lee at Appomattox, the fighting finally came close to Cahaba as General James H. Wilson's Federal forces defeated Confederate forces under the command of General Nathan Bedford Forrest at the Battle of Selma. After the battle, General Wilson sent a courier to General Forrest inviting him to a meeting to discuss an exchange of prisoners and other matters of mutual concern. General Forrest accepted, and the two generals met on April 8, 1865, at the old Crocheron Mansion in Cahaba, which was then owned by Colonel Thomas M. Mathews, a planter and Union sympathizer. General Wilson described the initial greetings as "reserved" but further noted that they dined over a "bountiful Southern dinner" and that by the end of the meal, "we were treating each other like old acquaintances." General Wilson had hoped that the result of their meeting would be a prisoner exchange due to the fact that he was burdened with approximately 2,400 prisoners taken during the Battle of Selma. General Forrest did not reject the proposal outright but indicated that he would have to receive approval from his superiors. That approval was not forthcoming, and General Wilson marched all of the prisoners to Montgomery, where he paroled them home.[114]

If indeed a prisoner exchange had been arranged as had been hoped by General Wilson, undoubtedly many prisoners from Castle Morgan would have avoided the disaster that struck the steamboat *Sultana*. Unfortunately, however, many of Castle Morgan's Union prisoners were transferred to a parole camp in Vicksburg, where they were joined by prisoners from the infamous Andersonville Prison in Georgia. At Vicksburg, approximately 2,300 of these prisoners were crammed aboard the *Sultana*, which was to take them north to Cairo, Illinois, where they were to be released to their homes. Disaster loomed, however, as the *Sultana* was rated for a maximum of only 376 passengers and crew. It has been advanced that the overcrowding was encouraged by the owners of the boat themselves because they were paid five dollars a head for each Union soldier jam-packed on board for the doomed trip. Conditions were so crowded that the soldiers could find no place to sleep and barely had enough space to stand. The *Sultana* almost capsized early in the voyage when hundreds of the men aboard rushed to one side of the boat to get into a picture being shot by a photographer on the shore. Its fate was sealed, however, when three of the steamboat's boilers exploded at about 2:00 a.m. on April 27, 1865, eight miles past Memphis. At least 1,700 people died as a result, either perishing in the blast or ensuing fire or drowning as they tried to escape from the burning steamship. It was not covered much in the media of the time due to the public's preoccupation with the assassination of President Abraham Lincoln just two weeks earlier. Nevertheless, this accident has since been recognized as the worst maritime disaster in U.S. history, even surpassing the sinking of the *Titanic* during its maiden voyage on April 14, 1912, when 1,517 people lost their lives.[115]

The close of the Civil War and the loss of the county seat to Selma brought about an exodus of most of Cahaba's white population as the emancipated

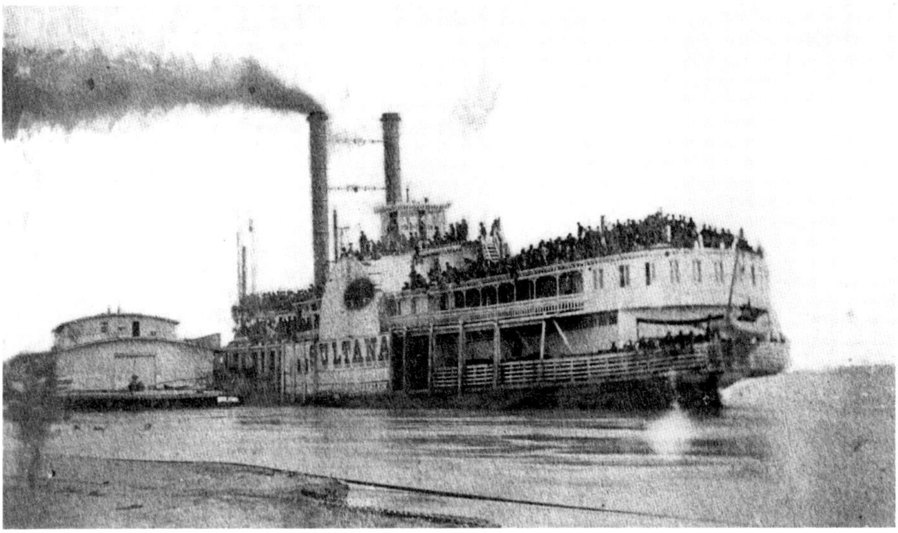

The *Sultana*, a steamboat transporting prisoners home from Castle Morgan, caught fire when three of its boilers exploded, killing some 1,700 people. *Wikimedia Commons.*

African American slaves used their newly acquired political power to gain control of the town through the ballot box. Many of the former slaves became landowners, including such families as the Lightnings, Lattimores and Arthurs. Others were active in politics, including Jordan Hatcher, who became Cahaba's postmaster; John Walker, one of Alabama's first black state legislators, who later became a successful lawyer and served as a trustee of Howard University in Washington, D.C.; and Jeremiah Haralson, who was the only African American to serve in the Alabama House of Representatives, Alabama Senate and the U.S. House of Representatives. As a result of these advancements, Cahaba became known as the "Mecca of the Radical Republican Party." Despite the modest political gains of the African American population, Cahaba was doomed when it was hit by another calamitous flood in 1865, and the county seat was moved to Selma in 1866. Thereafter, the town began closing up piece by piece, as many of the houses and stores were being torn down and sold for scrap or moved to Selma to be rebuilt. By 1870, the black population had dwindled down to only 302, with the white population barely holding on at approximately 120. In 1880, Cahaba was well on its way to becoming a ghost town when that year's census no longer recognized it as a town. By 1900, most of what was left of Cahaba was in ruins. A few African American families continued in the area until at least the 1950s. Also, a white family by the name of Kirkpatrick

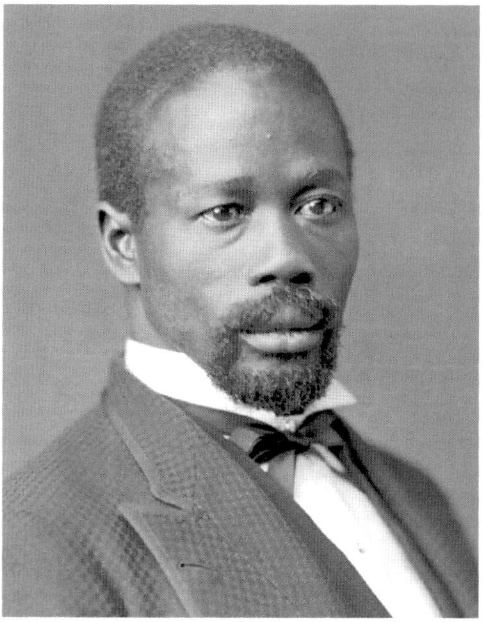

Jeremiah Haralson (1846–1916) of Dallas County was a successful black politician serving in the Alabama legislature and the U.S. House of Representatives during Reconstruction. *Library of Congress.*

managed a progressive farming operation known as Kirkview Farm until the 1930s.[116]

The days of Old Cahaba are gone forever. In her *Memories of Old Cahaba*, published in 1908, Anna Gayle Fry mourned the passing of those bygone days, which she had seen through rose-colored glasses, but she also appreciated the worth of the town's site despite the ruins:

> *Though long years have passed and the ruin is now perfect and complete, the site of the old town is still a lovely spot, where the pure, limpid waters gush unceasingly from the artesian wells; where the flowers planted long years ago still bloom in perennial spring in old-time yards; where the mocking bird still sings in springtime, and the Cherokee roses, full with blossoms, shed their snowy petals along the deserted streets...and the moon rises in its old-time splendor unfolding the ruined town in its soft, mellow light and lovingly shadows the graves of the dead who, when living, were among the most refined, cultivated, and intellectual people that ever adorned the State of Alabama.*[117]

Site of Cahaba Today

In the early 1900s, the site of Old Cahaba began to attract various archaeological and historical societies. In 1926, an organization known as the Cahaba Memorial Association organized riverboat pilgrimages to encourage preservation of the site's cemeteries, ruins and remaining structures. In the early 1940s, the state created the Cahaba Historical Commission to manage

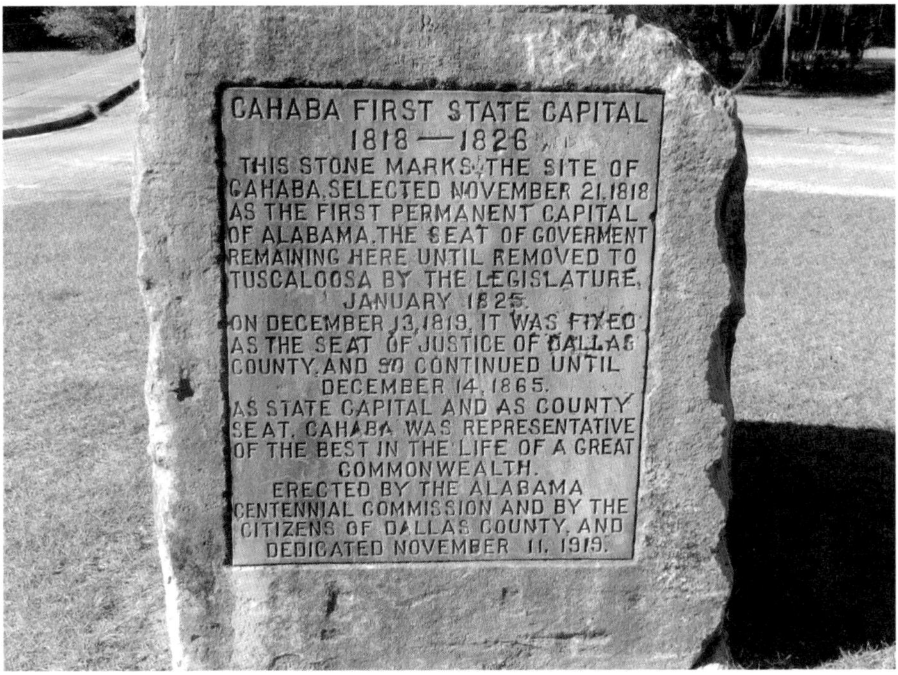

A stone marker commemorating the capital at Cahaba. *Taken by author.*

preservation projects there. However, with little authority and a lack of regular state funding, the commission was not in a position to prevent the mounting loss of structures to vandals and the elements. In 1973, the site was added to the National Register of Historic Places. Authority over the site finally was transferred officially in 1975 to the Alabama Historical Commission, which now maintains the site as the Old Cahawba Archaeological Site. The site includes a welcome center and education room, picnic area, hiking trails, interpretive signs and a nature trail. Today, visitors may observe old artesian wells, collapsed cellars, chimney ruins, old cemeteries and an impressive two-story brick residence that served as slave quarters for the old Kirkpatrick mansion. St. Luke's Episcopal Church, built in 1854 and moved away when the town died, has been returned to the site of Old Cahawba. Other attractions include the foundation of the Cahaba Federal Prison, where more than nine thousand Union soldiers were imprisoned during the Civil War, and the Crocheron Columns, today's most recognizable symbol of Cahaba's long-decayed mansions. This historical site is also centered between the entrance to the Black Belt Nature and Heritage Tourism Trail and the end of the Cahaba River Canoe Trail.[118]

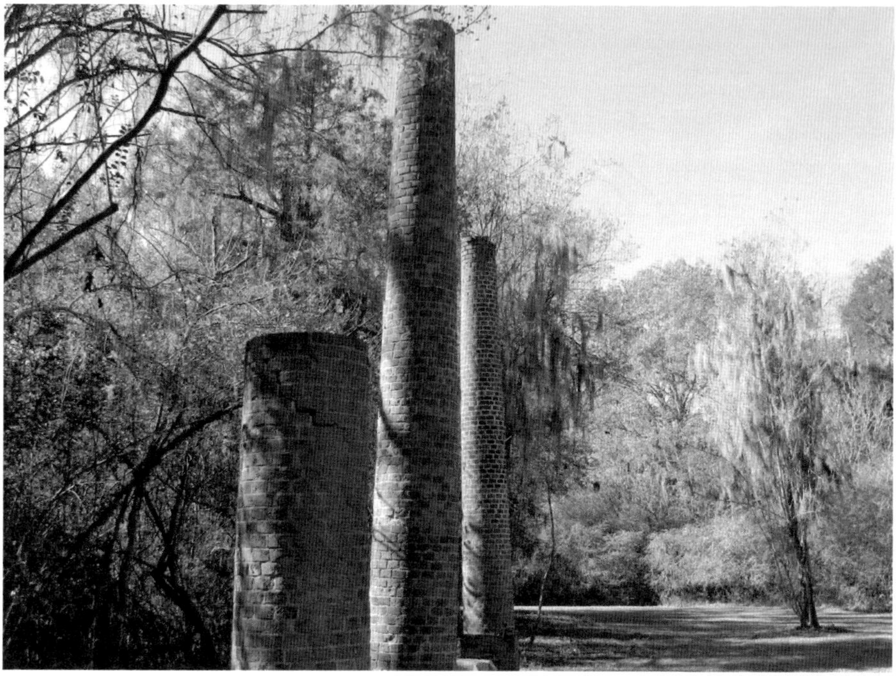

The Crocheron Columns, a modern-day symbol of Old Cahaba. *Taken by author.*

In 2008, a group of interested people founded the Cahaba Foundation, Inc. to serve as a fundraising arm primarily for land acquisition and archaeological exploration on the site. Daniel J. Meador, founder and first president of the foundation, set forth the mission of the foundation:

> *Old Cahawba was the birthplace of the state government and a flourishing antebellum center. Today it is deserted and ghostly, but rich in archaeological remains. Surrounded by two rivers, it is also rich in flora and fauna and unique biodiversity…This site should be preserved for posterity, and we invite everyone to join us in this effort.*

In September 2011, the foundation donated ten contiguous parcels of land totaling twenty-seven acres to the park and began a capital campaign to raise $2 million for a new visitor complex and two additional historic buildings. Today, the Alabama Historical Commission owns only 65 percent of the property. The property remaining in private hands—including the site of the Perrine Mansion and its world-famous artesian well—is owned by thirty-two different individuals. The Cahaba

Foundation is focusing its efforts on acquiring the remaining 35 percent of the land remaining under private ownership as quickly as it can in order to protect the site from private development and a loss of irreplaceable archaeological remains.[119]

CHAPTER 4
TUSCALOOSA

CAPITAL OF ALABAMA (1826–1846)

FORMATIVE PERIOD

The town of Tuscaloosa, which became Alabama's fourth capital, is located on the Black Warrior River in west-central Alabama. Originally referred to as the "Falls of the Black Warrior" or "Tuscaloosa Falls," *Tuscaloosa* means "Black Warrior" in the Choctaw language. Tuscaloosa (aka Tascaluza or Tuskalusa) was also the name of the imposing Indian chieftain whom de Soto defeated at the epic Battle of Mabila in 1540 during his expedition through Alabama. Chief Tascaluza was a late Mississippian period leader of a Muskogean-speaking tribe of Native Americans. He was described in a contemporaneous account of the expedition: "His appearance was full of dignity, he was tall of person, muscular, lean, and symmetrical. He was the suzerain of many territories, and of a numerous people, being equally feared by his vassals and the neighboring nations." It is believed that the members of this tribe were descendants of the earlier Mississippian mound builders who had established a large settlement less than twenty miles south of the present-day city of Tuscaloosa. The settlement, now known as Moundville, was situated along the banks of the Black Warrior River and first inhabited around AD 1120. The site consisted of over 325 acres and contained twenty-nine earthen mounds. By AD 1200, Moundville had emerged as a complex community with approximately one thousand people living behind its protective walls. Nevertheless, a large segment of Moundville society chose to live outside

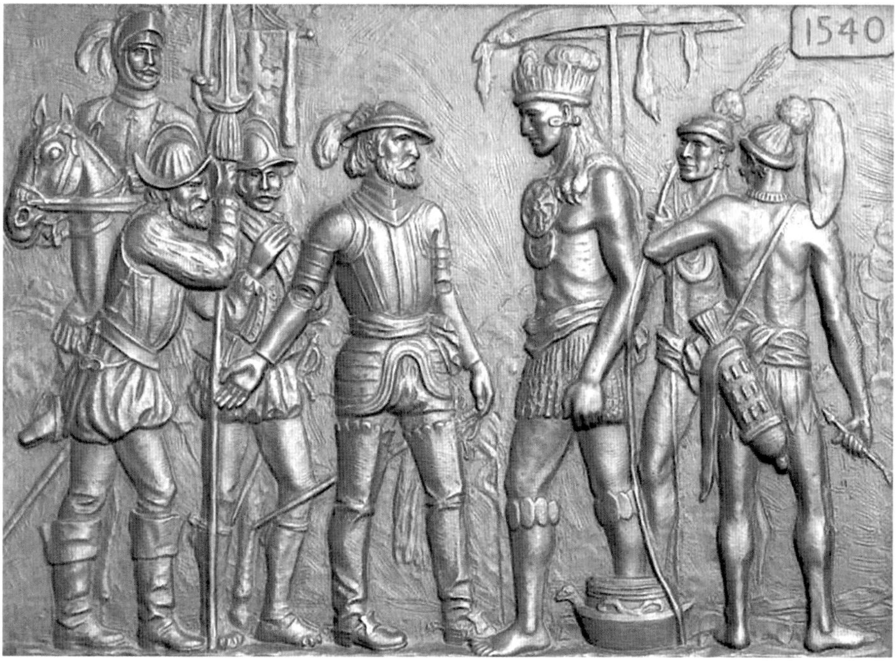

Mural of Chief Tuscaloosa meeting De Soto on the bronze door of the Alabama Department of Archives and History. *Library of Congress.*

the fortified town on farmsteads up and down the Black Warrior River, which certainly would have put some of them very close to the site of contemporary Tuscaloosa. Moundville began to decline about AD 1350, and by the 1500s, the town had been completely abandoned.[120]

Sometime during the seventeenth century, the Black Warrior River Valley became an uninhabited boundary between the Creeks to the east and the Choctaws to the west. George Strothers Gaines, who became the Indian Agent at St. Stephens in 1805, discovered that shortly after 1800, the Choctaws had allowed the Creeks to establish a village within the boundary area near the Falls of the Black Warrior. This future site of the city of Tuscaloosa was known to whites as Black Warrior's Town. Its chief was named Oce-oche-motla, meaning the "Full-Grown Warrior, Little Hickory." Twice a year, once in the spring and once in the fall, Chief Oce-oche-motla led a party of his warriors to the future territorial capital of St. Stephens to trade deerskins for powder, guns and other provisions as needed. After Tecumseh's visit to the area in the fall of 1811, Agent Gaines in St. Stephens began to see the increasing hostility of the Creeks, some of whom were from

Black Warrior's Town, as evidenced by their refusal to pay for large amounts of goods they had purchased on credit.[121]

Black Warrior's Town figured prominently in the increasing tensions that led to the Creek War of 1813–14, when a white woman by the name of Martha Crawley, from the Duck River region in Tennessee, was kidnapped in May 1813 by a party of Creek Indians returning from a visit with Tecumseh and the Shawnees. During this raid, several settlers were murdered, and Mrs. Crawley was taken hostage. After this raid, Mrs. Crawley was taken to several Creek towns until she was finally left with the Creeks at Black Warrior's Town, where she was held prisoner for several months. Mrs. Crawley's kidnapping and the murder of the white settlers enraged the inhabitants of the Old Southwest and was widely reported in the frontier press. Fortunately, however, Mrs. Crawley managed to escape from her captors and wound up with the family of George Strothers Gaines in St. Stephens; eventually, she was reunited with the remainder of her family.[122]

On August 30, 1813, a force of about 700 Creek warriors attacked and destroyed Fort Mims, located in present-day Baldwin County, where a group of Americans, United States–allied Creeks and African American slaves had fortified themselves in anticipation of a possible attack. The massacre of approximately 250 of the defenders, including civilian men, women and children, resulted in cries for revenge and calls to arms. Primary among those responding to the demands of an outraged public was General Andrew Jackson of Tennessee, who set out for Alabama in October 1813. After his troops crossed the Tennessee River at Ditto's Landing near Huntsville, General Jackson, perhaps in retaliation for the captivity of Mrs. Crawley, ordered Colonel John Coffee to take a force of about 600 cavalrymen to destroy Black Warrior's Town at the Falls of the Black Warrior. Although they found the town abandoned, Colonel Coffee ordered that all the empty cabins and tribal houses be burned to the ground. The legendary hero Davy Crockett was attached as a scout in Coffee's command and was present at the burning of Black Warrior's Town. In his autobiography, published in 1834, he gave the following account:

> *We pushed on till we got to what was called the Black Warrior's Town, which stood near the very spot where Tuscaloosa now stands, which is the seat of government for the state of Alabama. This Indian town was a large one; but when we arrived we found the Indians had all left it. There was a large field of corn standing out, and a pretty good supply in some cribs. There was also a fine quantity of dried leaves, which were very acceptable*

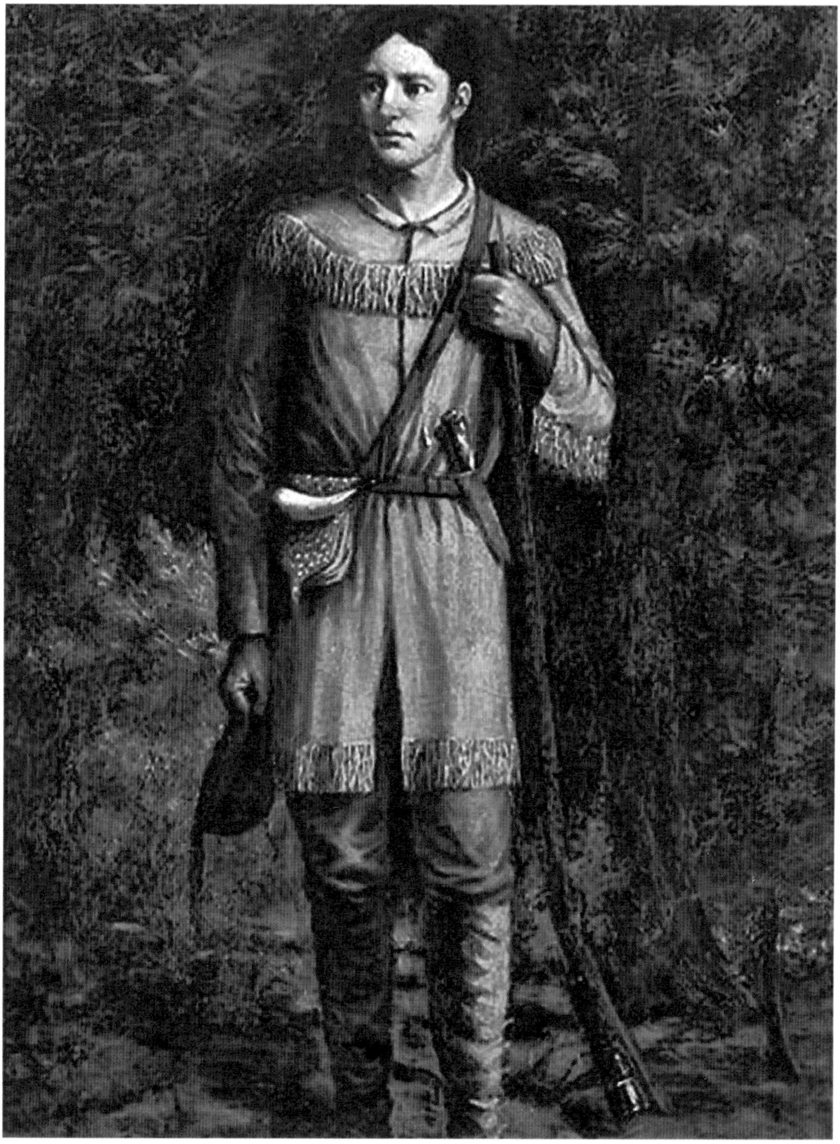

Davy Crockett (1786–1836) accompanied forces directed by General Andrew Jackson to destroy Black Warrior's Town at the Falls of the Black Warrior. *Wikimedia Commons.*

> *to us; and without delay we secured them as well as the corn, and then burned the town to ashes; after which we left the place. In the field where we gathered the corn we saw plenty of fresh Indian tracks, and we had no doubt they had been scared off by our arrival.*[123]

General Jackson's forces thereafter continued their march through Alabama, finally defeating the Creek Nation at the Battle of Horseshoe Bend on March 27, 1814. The resulting Treaty of Fort Jackson brought about the cession of approximately twenty-two million acres of land by the Creeks. This cession opened up Alabama for settlement. With the push westward, white settlers soon entered the area in and around what would become Tuscaloosa. Ironically, Davy Crockett was among the first to come into the area looking for a spot to settle. Shortly after the Creek War, Crockett's first wife died. Then living in Franklin County, Tennessee, near the Alabama border, Crockett remarried and, in the fall of 1815, joined two of his neighbors to look for a place where they could relocate their families. On their journey into Alabama, one of the neighbors had to be left behind when he was bitten by a poisonous snake. Crockett and the other neighbor then "passed through a large rich valley, called Jones Valley, where several other families had settled, and continued their course till we came near to the place where Tuscaloosa now stands." While camped at this location, their horses got away from them. Crockett gave chase through rough terrain and became seriously ill. He was discovered by some Indians and was eventually taken to a house near present-day Bessemer, Alabama, to recover. Soon, Crockett was able to return to Tennessee to his wife and thus ended his search for a place to settle near the Falls of the Black Warrior. Tuscaloosa historian Matthew Clinton observed, "But for the accident of his horses running away and his sickness Davy Crockett might have been Tuscaloosa's first settler."[124]

Since Davy Crockett's home-seeking trip to the Falls of the Black Warrior did not pan out, he left the door open for someone else to have the distinction of becoming the first permanent white settler of Tuscaloosa. Who that person was, however, has not been wholly agreed on by historians of that time, although in all probability it was Thomas York, due to the consensus of opinions among prominent early settlers such as Judge Washington Moody, Dr. John L. Tendall and Samuel Meek. Arriving shortly after Thomas York were Jonathan and Emanuel York, who were thought to be his sons. Tradition within the Meek family was that their first house in Tuscaloosa had been the home of Thomas York, to whom they referred as Tuscaloosa's first settler. York arrived at the Falls of the Black Warrior from Tennessee by way of Blount County, Alabama, in the winter or spring of 1816, just in time to plant a crop of corn that year. Not long after the arrival of the Yorks came John Barton, a blacksmith; Patrick Scott; Josiah Tilley; and John G. Ring.

The Yorks, as well as other original settlers, stayed in Tuscaloosa only a few years before moving on. Thomas York and John Barton moved to nearby Jones Valley, while Jonathan York, Josiah Tilley and John G. Ring moved to Pickens County. Typical of the westward movement at that time, Tilley left Pickens County in 1830 and headed to Texas.[125]

Another early settler who did not stay in Tuscaloosa very long was Gideon Lincecum, a pioneer of some renown. Lincecum and his father set out for the "Alabama, Black Warrior, Tombecbee, and Chattahoochie countries" in March 1818 in pursuit of their love for a "border life." They reached Tuscaloosa in the late spring of 1818. Lincecum built "a little clapboard house on the river side of town," while his father and his family settled eight miles below Tuscaloosa. Gideon Lincecum said of Tuscaloosa, "It was at that time a small log cabin village; but people from Tennessee were arriving daily, and in the course of that year it grew to be a considerable town." Earlier, in 1817, Hiram Cochrane had arrived in Tuscaloosa, which "presented nothing as a village but a rude cluster of log huts, heterogeneously arranged, with little regard to regularity as to streets." After reporting that the area was settling very quickly, the *Niles Weekly Register* for February 28, 1818, added that the "Black Warrior River, which is called the 'Nile of the Western country' is spoken of as the great outlet for the products of this interesting part of the republic. A town has been established immediately below the falls of this river, which, though a wilderness ten years ago, now contains, by a late census, two hundred and ninety-six inhabitants."[126]

When Thomas York arrived in 1816, the Falls of the Black Warrior was within Washington County, which had been created in 1800 as a political subdivision of the Mississippi Territory. The county seat was located some 250 miles away in St. Stephens, the future territorial capital of Alabama. It included most of present-day Alabama, except for the territory south of the thirty-first parallel, which was obtained from Spain in 1813. Alabama became a territory in 1817, and its first territorial legislature passed an act creating Tuscaloosa County on February 7, 1818. The act creating the county also provided for a judicial system to serve its needs. It was not until December 13, 1819, that the new state legislature enacted a bill incorporating the town of Tuscaloosa (at that time spelled "Tuskaloosa") just one day before Alabama was admitted to the Union. This act of incorporation set up a commission form of government for Tuscaloosa with seven commissioners to be elected by "every free white male of the age of twenty one years" and a president to be chosen among the commissioners so elected.[127]

A little over a year after its incorporation, Tuscaloosa was presented with a rival town just a few blocks to the west of it with the incorporation of what was awkwardly called the "Lower Part of the Town of Tuscaloosa" (shortened to the "New Town of Tuscaloosa" and later known simply as "Newtown"). The incorporation of Newtown was the result of land being granted by Congress to the Connecticut Deaf and Dumb Asylum for the purpose of allowing it to raise funds. William H. Ely, purchasing agent for the asylum, bought up the land that would become Newtown, thereby inhibiting the growth of Tuscaloosa and earning the wrath of Tuscaloosans. Since Newtown was surveyed before Tuscaloosa, it grew much faster, so much so that in 1822, the citizens voted to move the county seat from Tuscaloosa to Newtown. Newtown prospered for a while, with a number of businesses located on its main thoroughfare. Near the river were situated a cigar factory, a sawmill and a warehouse. Tuscaloosa, however, eventually prevailed as the predominant town when it became the state capital in 1826 and was authorized by the General Assembly to annex Newtown. Thereafter, Newtown no longer existed as a separate town. On March 4, 1842, a tornado ripped through Tuscaloosa, destroying many of the town's original structures and hitting the Newtown section particularly hard.[128]

While Alabama was still a territory, Tuscaloosa County was represented in the territorial General Assembly by Julius Sims, and its first sheriff was John Smith. The first justice of the county court was Isaac Patrick, and the first clerk of that court was Matthew Click. Marmaduke Williams, who would later challenge William Wyatt Bibb to be Alabama's first state governor, and Dr. John L. Tindall, one of Tuscaloosa's first physicians, represented the county in the Constitutional Convention of 1819 held in Huntsville. Other prominent persons in early Tuscaloosa included merchants and businessmen such as Levin Powell, John and Matthew Click, Captain James H. Dearing, Henry A. Snow, George Morgan and Charles M. Foster. Physicians, in addition to John L. Tendall, included Jeptha V. Isbell, William Purris, Thomas Hunter, Robert L. Kennon, Samuel M. Meek, Nicholas Perkins and Reuben Searcy, who was later named president of the board of trustees of the Alabama Insane Hospital (later Bryce Hospital). Although early Alabama historian Willis Brewer states that William L. Adams was the first lawyer to come to Tuscaloosa, he also indicates that Sion L. Perry, a veteran of the Creek War of 1813–14, was "the first lawyer who settled within the limits of the town of Tuskaloosa." Other early prominent attorneys included Constantine Perkins, who was elected as Tuscaloosa County's district solicitor in 1819 and Alabama's attorney general in 1825; Seth

Barton, who later moved to New Orleans and was appointed ambassador to Venezuela by President John Knox Polk; Harvey W. Ellis, who first practiced in Newtown but later moved to Tuscaloosa, where he was elected to the legislature five times; Judge Henry W. Minor, who became a justice on the Alabama Supreme Court and later became its clerk; and Henry W. Collier, who served as chief justice of the Alabama Supreme Court and was elected as the state's fourteenth governor in 1849.[129]

The census taken for Tuscaloosa in 1820 revealed a population of 5,894 white and 2,335 African Americans, most of whom were slaves. An earlier census in 1818 had revealed a total population of only "two hundred and ninety-six inhabitants" who lived in a village of log huts. Even in 1821, a traveler passing through Tuscaloosa observed, "The town was little more than hewn out of the woods. Piles of brick and timber crowded the main, indeed the only street of the place, and denoted the rawness and poverty of the region." The traveler complained that he lodged in the only hotel in town and was forced to share a room with two other people. An even more damning description was provided by New Englander William H. Ely, the purchasing agent for the Connecticut Asylum. When he was in Tuscaloosa during 1820 and 1821, he reported that there were "about 20 stores & little Groceries, or Hucksters Shops." He also noted that "what they call their houses, are either the most despicable rough dirty & uncomfortable rolling log cabins, or less durable & more mean buildings; most of them without a single Pane of Glass, with scarcely a saw'd board or Plank, Nail or any other Iron about them." As for the inhabitants, Ely observed that they were generally thoughtless in their dress, lacking in serious religious instruction and prone to heavy drinking. He described their teachers as ignorant and immoral, their women as unread and "much of the white Population of the State are extremely indolent, either too proud, or too lazy to work, or even think." He stereotyped the men as spending their days at taverns, gambling houses, horse races and cockfights. He also asserted that brazen crimes were committed and were ignored by local law enforcement. While some of his observations were undoubtedly accurate, Ely nevertheless painted with a very broad brush and exhibited an obvious New England bias against the more rustic frontier of the Old Southwest.[130]

Despite Ely's condemnation of Tuscaloosa and its citizens, between 1820 and 1826, the soon-to-be next capital of Alabama was developing into a more sophisticated town. Ely revealed that there were already approximately twenty stores in 1820. There were numerous lawyers and physicians. Tuscaloosa's first newspaper, the *Tuscaloosa Republican*, was established in 1819. Within a year, its name was changed to Tuscaloosa's *American Mirror* and continued under that name until 1827, a year after Tuscaloosa became the state's fourth capital. Tuscaloosa's fledgling economy got a tremendous boost when the first steamboat made it up the Warrior River all the way from Mobile in 1821. The *Cotton Plant* steamboat left Mobile on December 5, 1821, and arrived in Tuscaloosa fifteen days later, on December 21, 1821. The boat had a thirty-horsepower engine and an eighty-ton capacity. On its return trip to Mobile, which took only nine days, the *Cotton Plant* carried 330 bales of cotton. Sometime during the spring of 1822, a second steamboat named the *Tombigbee* reached Tuscaloosa. The *Tombigbee* had been built in Blakely, Alabama, by Captain James H. Dearing. When the *Tombigbee* made its maiden voyage upriver from St. Stephens, Dearing brought along his family and goods to Tuscaloosa. Dearing became one of Tuscaloosa's most prominent early citizens. In addition to operating steamboats, he ran steam mills and engaged in farming. He was also a director of the State Bank and served in the legislature. In 1834, he built a mansion on the main avenue leading to present-day downtown Tuscaloosa. This house later served as the governor's residence during Arthur Bagby's term. In 1946, the University Club was established there as a private club for University of Alabama faculty and staff. The club is still operational and serves as a historical landmark for the city of Tuscaloosa and the University of Alabama.[131]

William Ely's assertion that the citizens of Tuscaloosa were not too serious about religion and lacked in religious instruction was contradicted by the fact that the major Christian denominations were diligent in establishing their churches in early Tuscaloosa. The Baptists were first to organize a congregation in January 1818, with four different pastors serving their first church between 1818 and 1827. In the summer of 1818, the first Methodist circuit-rider preacher came to Tuscaloosa and preached his first sermon in a tavern. Shortly thereafter, the Tuscaloosa Circuit was established. About this same time, four Methodists ministers, who were also physicians, arrived in Tuscaloosa, and in 1824, the Methodist church in Tuscaloosa was made a full-time station. The Catholic Church held an organizational meeting in 1819 but did not have a resident priest until 1844. On May 6, 1820, the Presbyterians of Tuscaloosa were organized by Reverend Andrew Brown of the South Carolina Presbytery. They first met in a church in Newtown but later relocated to Tuscaloosa. Although the Episcopalian Church did not organize in Tuscaloosa until January 1828, it was only the second Episcopalian congregation to organize in Alabama.[132]

When 1826 arrived, Tuscaloosa was ready to take over the reins of government from Cahawba. Tuscaloosa's prominent and influential citizens, as well as its supporters from the Tennessee Valley, had fought hard to acquire the state capital for the Druid City. Tuscaloosa just squeaked by, however, with a one-vote margin of victory in the senate. John "Red" Brown of Jefferson County and a known supporter of Tuscaloosa, saved the day for Tuscaloosa when he upset John Wood, the incumbent of the Jefferson County senate seat who was believed to be opposed to relocating the capital to Tuscaloosa. Wood filed an unsuccessful challenge to the election, and Brown was declared to be the legal senator representing Jefferson County. With the challenge rejected, Brown proceeded to cast his vote in favor of Tuscaloosa, thereby securing a favorable outcome in the senate by just one vote. When the House passed the relocation bill with a more comfortable margin on December 13, 1825, the state capital was on the road once again to a new site.[133]

Tuscaloosa Serves as State Capital (1826–1846)

The state government convened in Tuscaloosa for the first time on November 20, 1826. Since no permanent capitol building had been constructed yet, the 1826 session of the General Assembly met in the Bell Tavern, which had hurriedly been enlarged and reconfigured to accommodate the legislature. The tavern, later renamed the Washington Hotel, was located at the intersection of present-day University Boulevard and Twenty-second Avenue. It housed the General Assembly for just one session until a more convenient temporary structure was made available. The temporary accommodation was a wood-frame building located on Broad Street several blocks to the west of the Bell Tavern. Legislative sessions were held there until 1829. In anticipation of a permanent structure to house state government, a resolution was passed by both houses of the General Assembly on December 14, 1826, authorizing a committee of five members from the House and a like number from the senate to identify potential sites for the location of a permanent capitol building. The committee identified five potential sites for the General Assembly as a whole to consider. After three ballots, members of the House and senate finally gave a majority of their votes to a site known as Childress' Hill. This site was undoubtedly chosen because it was located at the end of Broad Street, which put it near the center of Tuscaloosa and Newtown, as well as being near the river. This site had been cleared originally in 1816 by William Wilson, one of Tuscaloosa's earliest white settlers. Wilson and Major James Childress bought parts of the property at a public auction in 1821. When Childress built a log cabin on his portion of the land, the site became known as Childress' Hill.[134]

Still meeting in temporary quarters described by some as a "shabby old tenement" resembling a "gin-house," on January 3, 1827, the General Assembly ordered that plans for a statehouse, which had been reported to it by the joint committee, be referred to a select committee "with instructions to report any alteration in the same they may think necessary, and to report such instructions to the commissioners appointed to contract for the building of said state house as they may deem proper." The first design of the capitol did not gain universal approval, as demonstrated by one critic who proclaimed that if a structure were built pursuant to the original plans, it would "have more the appearance of a dutch barn or a cotton factory than a State Capitol." Much more serious than derogatory comments concerning the design of the capitol was the continued opposition of those in south Alabama who opposed the construction of any permanent statehouse in Tuscaloosa. Despite artistic critics and relocation foes, the commissioners overseeing the capitol's construction placed advertisements in the state's leading newspapers for a building superintendent and proposals for construction of the capitol building. In February 1827, the commissioners chose William Nichols, who had recently remodeled North Carolina's capitol in Raleigh.[135]

Nichols arrived in Tuscaloosa in the spring of 1827 and was quick to discover the defects in the commissioner's capitol plan. Although construction was delayed until the next legislative session while the plans were being revised by Nichols, the building commissioners went ahead and contracted for stone and brick, which would be needed regardless of what design changes were to be made. In November 1827, Nichols, restrained by only $40,000 having been appropriated for construction, submitted a revised plan that allowed for a nice-looking, but small, capitol. Due to the lack of sufficient space, Nichols's revised plan was rejected, and he was asked to present plans for a larger structure along with an estimate of its cost. Nichols then submitted plans that would increase the size of the building by one-fourth and cost an extra $15,000. Submitted with these plans was an explanatory letter to the legislative committee in which he stated, "In obedience to the direction of the committee of the Senate on the State Capitol I have enlarged the plans, so as to give comfortable accommodation to the Legislative departments and Supreme Court, that the apartments were before too limited must be attributed to the bounds prescribed by the amount of the appropriation."[136]

A joint resolution of the General Assembly approved Nichols's plans on December 20, 1827. That plan indicated that the general form of the building was that of a cross-shaped structure. The main feature of the design of the exterior was an impressive dome that could be seen from quite a distance. A contemporaneous account described the exterior of the building as "grand, imposing and striking in its proportions, and productive of the most pleasing sensations to the cultivated mind." The interior of the building was even more majestic with its spacious halls, which contained the two houses of the General Assembly on the main floor of the north (senate) and south (House) wings. These two wings were joined by a rotunda in the center of the building. The Alabama Supreme Court was housed on the ground floor in the western arm of the "cruciform." The entrance vestibule was located in the eastern arm and included two spectacular curving flights of stairs leading up to the principal floor housing the General Assembly. Executive offices, including those of the governor and secretary of state, were located on the ground floor in the southern wing, and those of the treasurer and comptroller were located on that floor's north wing.[137]

As the capitol appeared to be nearing completion in 1829, enthusiastic townspeople decided to hold a Fourth of July celebration on the grounds of the new capitol. Although the capitol would not be completely finished for almost two more years, by November 1829, it was well enough along for the General Assembly to meet there for the 1829–30 session. The total cost when completed was approximately $150,000, well above the $55,000 that Nichols had projected. Accordingly, in December 1829, Nichols was accused of mismanagement of funds. The building commissioners later rejected these charges as being the result of hostile chatter among disgruntled unsuccessful applicants for contracts. That Nichols's work was appreciated despite the cost overruns is evidenced by Governor John Murphy's address on November 17, 1829, wherein he noted that the "taste, skill, and experience of the Architect, Captain Nichols, deserved the highest commendations." This gubernatorial address, made while painting and plastering was still ongoing in other parts of the building, was the first delivered in the new capitol. Governor Murphy further remarked that he hoped that the capitol would "long remain a monument of the liberal ambition" and "long remain the council hall, and citadel of liberty."[138]

With the completion of the statehouse, Tuscaloosa had to adjust to its status as capital of Alabama. An account of life in the new capital by James

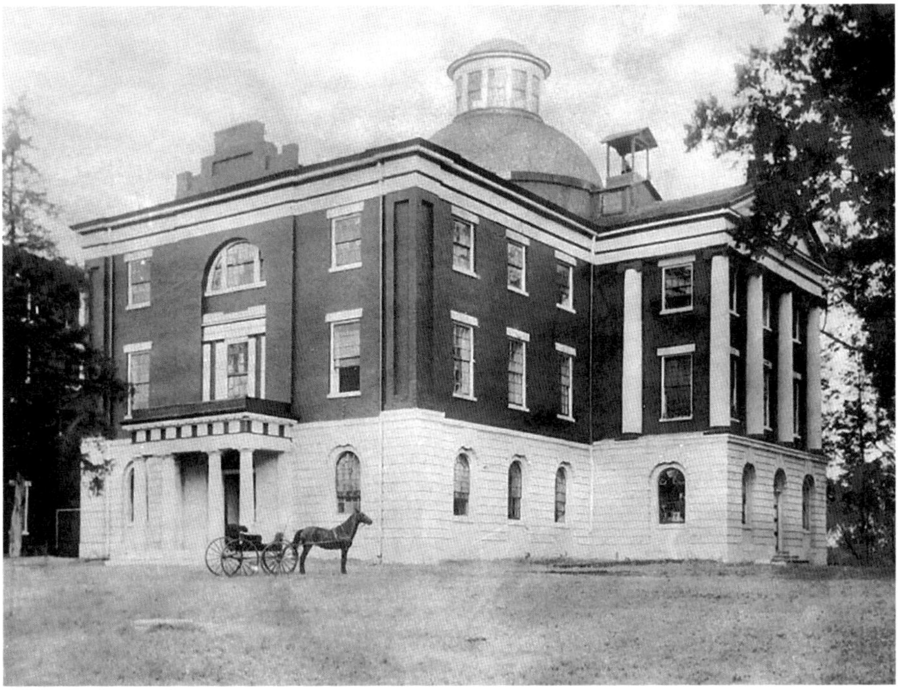

Tuscaloosa's capitol, constructed at a total cost of $150,000, was sufficiently complete for the General Assembly to meet there in November 1829. *Library of Congress.*

A. Anderson portrays a "sleepy old town" taking on "new life." This account indicates that the "town rapidly became the hub of Alabama's society circle, for there were assembled the wives and daughters of senators and supreme court judges, as well as numerous pleasure seekers and votaries of fashion from every part of the state." The account further observes that balls, card games, clubs and theater gatherings "occupied so much time that there was no time left for church going and religious worship." This, Anderson's account's continued, resulted in the "morality of Tuscaloosa rapidly declining." Anderson further recounted that "[g]amblers and men of leisure flocked to the place and the town quickly changed from a dreamy river town to a modern city of fashion and gaiety." To accommodate these men of leisure, gambling houses, saloons, theaters and restaurants "sprang up like magic and life in Tuscaloosa during those years that the town remained the state capital was one round of amusement, dissipation, and high carnival." According to this one account, the "season of dissipation and fast life" in Tuscaloosa was unsurpassed by any of the other capitals of Alabama.[139]

In 1831, Tuscaloosa was not only the capital of the state but also the home of the University of Alabama. The university opened its doors for the first time on April 17, 1831, after years of delay primarily because it was used as a political football when it was empowered by the General Assembly to sell lands and to invest the proceeds in a state bank. Governor Israel Pickens had delayed the debate for the location of the university to ensure that it would not need funds for construction until after it had invested $100,000 in the state bank. In any event, the stylish new campus, which was designed and constructed by William Nichols, who had built the state capitol, was finally completed. The central part of the campus was the Rotunda, which housed the library and a natural history collection, while its ground floor consisted of an auditorium used for chapel services and commencement exercises. The remainder of the campus consisted of the Lyceum, where classes were held; two dormitories; two faculty houses; and a dining room.[140]

Most of those enrolling in the university at this time were the boisterous sons of wealthy planters who were involved in a running battle of defiance against the university's first president, Alva Woods, an austere New Englander who was Harvard graduate and an ordained Baptist minister. Woods's New

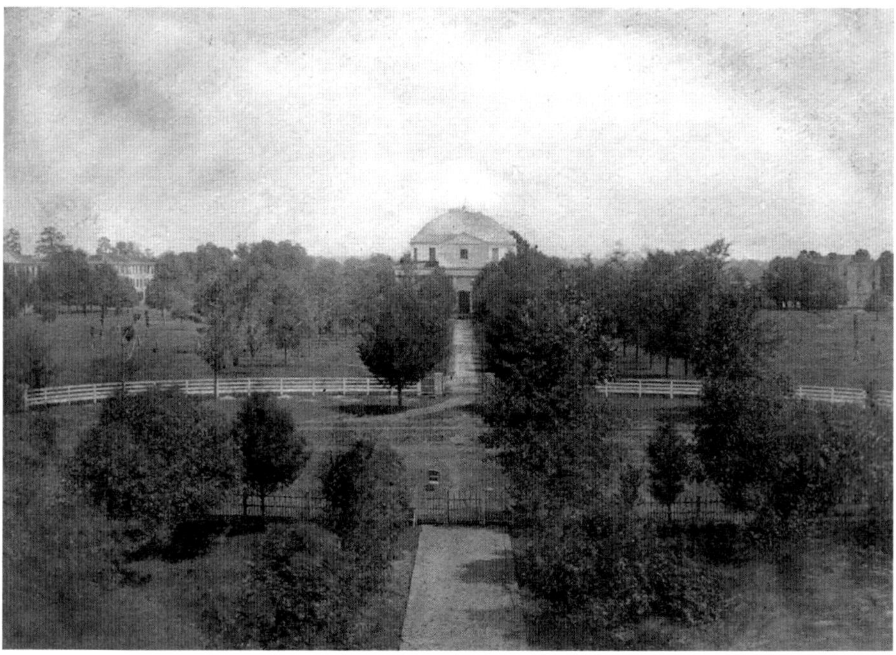

An 1859 photograph of the University of Alabama before it was burned by Federal forces in April 1865. *Courtesy University Libraries Division of Special Collections, the University of Alabama.*

England background had not prepared him for this rowdy frontier student body. One student rebellion after another erupted in response to Woods's autocratic rule. There were some very minor infractions of discipline, but drinking and gambling led to more serious infractions. For example, one student was expelled for assaulting a professor with a deadly weapon, while another was sent home for stabbing another student. Historian James Sellers describes the student body as "proud possessors of dirks, pistols, and bowie knives" who "could quickly and easily turn a roughhouse into an assault, or a student mass meeting into a mob." Woods did not back down to the students but eventually tired of the situation and resigned in December 1837. Before leaving with his family for providence Rhode Island, Woods served as the president of the board of trustees of the Tuscaloosa Female Athenaeum, which he had been instrumental in founding in 1836. Taking over as president of the university was Basil Manly, who was instrumental in the founding of what became Furman University. Although student unrest did not completely dissipate with Woods's departure, Manly, a southerner, was able to develop a better rapport with the student body during his term as president over the next eighteen years.[141]

Although the university was composed of a generally rowdy student body, its literary societies also produced a talented cadre of young writers under the tutelage of Professor Henry W. Hilliard. Professor Hilliard was a remarkable character possessing multiple talents as a lawyer, scholar, preacher, editor, politician and orator. A native of North Carolina, Hilliard was admitted to the bar in Georgia in 1829, but in 1831, he accepted an appointment to chair the English Department at the University of Alabama. The group of writers inspired by Hilliard's talent for teaching included William Russell Smith, Alexander Beaufort Meek and Albert A. Muller. William Russell Smith, called by some the "Father of Alabama Literature," later referred to this group as the "Tuskaloosa Bards" in his autobiography. As members of the university's Erosophic Society headed by Professor Hilliard, the group focused on politics, oratory and literature. Smith had the distinction of publishing the first literary periodical in the state, as well as the first play written by an Alabamian to be performed by a professional acting troupe. Alexander Beaufort Meek, a lawyer and newspaper editor, in addition to being a poet, would later publish an epic poem pertaining to the Creek War: *The Red Eagle: A Poem of the South.* Muller, an Episcopal rector while attending the university, published a few poems before leaving both the school and the church due to undisclosed "lapses from religion and morality." Jeremiah Clemens, a cousin of Samuel Clemens (Mark Twain) and a future U.S.

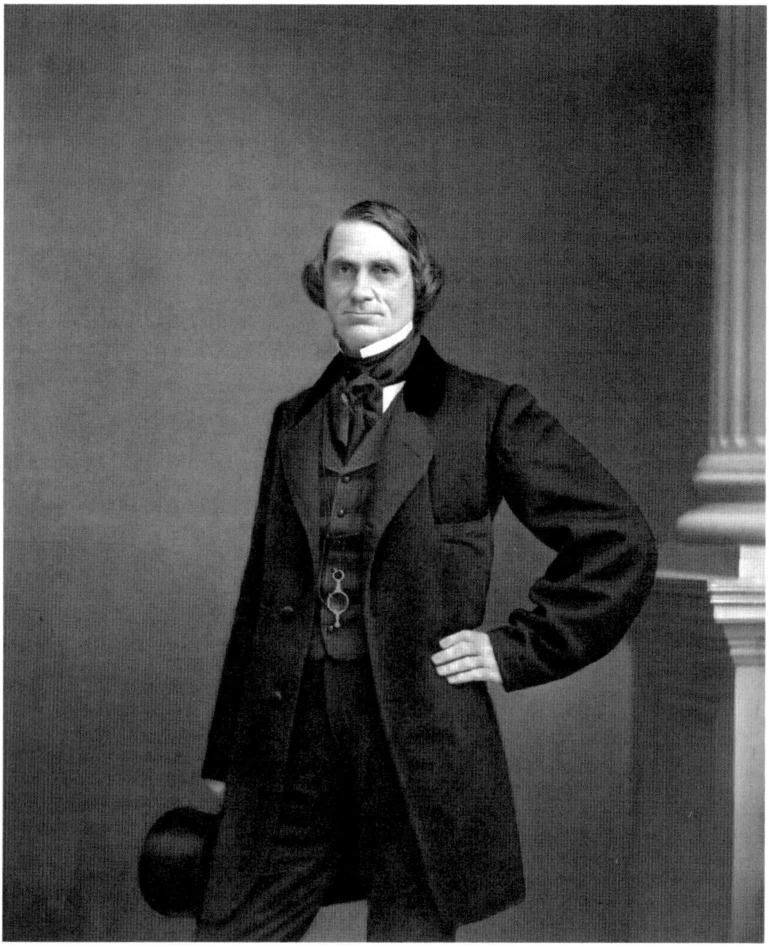

Professor Henry W. Hilliard (1808–1892) mentored a talented cadre of young writers later referred to as the "Tuscaloosa Bards." *Courtesy Alabama Department of Archives and History.*

senator, was not part of the Bards initially, but he was considered a member because four historical novels written later in his life were inspired by his association with the group. The collective efforts of Hilliard and his students earned Tuscaloosa the designation as the "literary capital" of Alabama during the 1830s and the early 1840s, during which time it was the state's seat of government.[142]

The January 19, 1831 issue of Tuscaloosa's *Alabama State Intelligencer* is reflective of a town a bit more cultured than one might surmise from the frequent rowdy demonstrations by the students of the university within its confines. This issue of the *Intelligencer* demonstrated that female education was progressing more placidly within the same town as the university, which was open only to males. The *Intelligencer* contained an announcement pertaining to the Tuscaloosa Female Academy, which preceded the Tuscaloosa Female Athenaeum by a number of years. The announcement was devoted to dispelling rumors that there was no female school in operation in Tuscaloosa by publicizing the union between the Tuscaloosa Female Education Society and the Sims' Female Academy. It further announced that the first session of the academy had commenced on January 6, 1831. In addition to a female academy, a dancing school was advertised to open as soon as a sufficient number of pupils, including both "young ladies and gentlemen," applied for instruction. It was further proclaimed that during lessons, "good order and decorum will be strictly observed." There was also notice in this issue of the *Intelligencer* that the first installment of rent was immediately due and payable on all pews let in the Episcopalian church. Also advertised for sale were *Henry's Commentaries*, which were described as an "Exposition of the Old and New Testament," with summaries of their chapters and commentaries provided by the Reverend Matthew Henry, a notable eighteenth-century British theologian. These two notices suggest that religion was not completely ignored, as implied by James Anderson in his description of Tuscaloosa during its capital years. Nonetheless, the paper advertised plenty of whiskey for sale and gave notice of the last cotillion of the season.[143]

An evolving Tuscaloosa would serve as the state's capital for twenty years. It soon became the target for lobbyists, who were already, at this early time in our history, converging on the state capital to push their various agendas. James Anderson put it this way: "Professional lobbyists appeared at the convening of every session of the legislature as regularly as the swallows make their appearance with the coming of spring." He further stated that they came from every portion of the state, "each with some bill in his pocket as he wanted passed on or with a knife up his sleeve to prune some bill that was antagonistic to the interests which he represented." John Murphy of Monroe County was the first of nine governors to serve during Tuscaloosa's reign as state capital. The others who served as governor during this time period were Gabriel Moore of Madison County (1829–31), Samuel B. Moore of Jackson County (1831), John Gayle of Green County (1831–35), Clement C. Clay of Madison County (1835–37), Hugh McVay of Lauderdale County (1837), Arthur P. Bagby of Monroe County (1837–41), Benjamin Fitzpatrick of Autauga County (1841–45) and Joshua L. Martin of Tuscaloosa County (1845–49). Governors serving in Huntsville and Cahaba had focused on organizing a

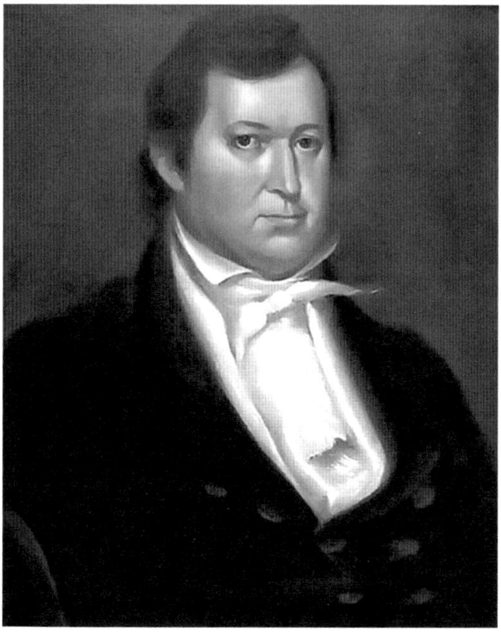

Governor John Murphy (1786–1841) was the first of nine governors to serve during Tuscaloosa's reign as state capital (1826–46). *Wikipedia Commons.*

state government and providing the basic necessities of safety and security to their citizens. In addition to local issues, the governors serving in Tuscaloosa began to focus on national issues such as tariffs, internal improvements, slavery, Indian policy and states' rights.[144]

Banking issues and the eventual closure of the State Bank of Alabama dominated local politics while the capital was in Tuscaloosa. In November 1826, Governor Murphy, in his address to the first General Assembly to meet in Tuscaloosa, warned of dangers posed to the State Bank of Alabama by the proposal of the Bank of the United States (BUS) to establish a branch bank in Mobile. Murphy was particularly concerned that the BUS would generate competition that would be harmful to the operations of Alabama's state bank. He therefore urged the legislature and the congressional delegation to take all appropriate actions in opposition to the establishment of a branch of the BUS in Mobile as "an invasion of our sovereignty." Despite this opposition, a branch of the BUS was located in Mobile. A decade later, Governor Arthur P. Bagby outlined what he considered flaws in the state banking system. In this regard, he called into question the number of officers and directors needed, the method of appointing them and their mode of compensation. This was amid allegations that directors received undue privileges and preferences with respect to loan accommodations and the payment of specie. In December 1837, the tarnished image of the state bank was brought into more focus as a result of excessive electioneering for directorship positions. Assistant clerk of the House of Representatives William Garrett described how legislators' votes were sought by enticing them with excellent cigars, fine liquors, oyster suppers and "other entertainments." Most of Governor Bagby's suggested reforms were ignored, but he did manage to obtain legislative approval of his recommendation to reduce the number of directors for each bank. Benjamin Fitzpatrick became governor in 1841 after a campaign in which he emphasized his anti-banking Jacksonian position. During the 1842 session of the General Assembly, state bank branches in Mobile, Decatur, Montgomery and Huntsville were abruptly liquidated. Only the main branch in Tuscaloosa survived, and it only had the power to purchase bills of exchange to pay toward the reduction of the state's indebtedness. Amid allegations of fraud and corruption, and because of gross mismanagement at the hands of the well-to-do and politically influential, the State Bank of Alabama's charter was not renewed by the legislature when it expired on January 1, 1845, and Alabama was without a state bank for the first time since 1823.[145]

Events with more national ramifications during Tuscaloosa's capital years included a clash with the federal government over the management of ceded Indians lands and the Creek War of 1836. With regard to the clash with the federal government, in 1833, President Andrew Jackson sent Frances Scott Key, author of "The Star-Spangled Banner" and federal prosecutor, to Alabama to negotiate a truce between the state and federal governments. The two governments had been sparring over the management of lands ceded by the Creek Nation to the United States as a result of the Treaty of Cusetta of 1832. The dispute was over white settlers encroaching on lands before the Creeks wishing to stay in Alabama could choose their allotments of land. Several violent incidents involving local citizens and federal troops had led to the necessity of peace negotiations. Cooler heads prevailed, partly due to Key's diplomatic efforts with Alabama governor John Gayle. Despite the resolution of this problem, another war with the Creeks broke out in 1836 during the governorship of Clement Comer Clay, who took personal command of the state militia during this crisis. Left in a desperate economic state after trading their allotments to speculators for pennies on the dollar, approximately three thousand Creeks joined in a final revolt against white settlers in the eastern section of Alabama. Federal troops, Alabama militia and seven hundred friendly Creeks put down this violent outbreak. The last major battle of this short-lived war took place in March 1837 at Hobdy's Bridge on the Pea River, located near Louisville in Barbour County. There, Alabama volunteers under General William Wellborn attacked and defeated a party of Creeks finding refuge in nearby swamps as they moved toward Florida. Afterward, approximately two thousand were rounded up as prisoners and sent to Montgomery, where they would begin their long trek to Oklahoma, as the "Trail of Tears" was tragically underway.[146]

With the end of these hostilities, Alabama was hit hard by the Panic of 1837. As land speculation ran rampant, the nation's economic bubble burst. To make matters worse, President Jackson's veto of the extension of the Bank of the United States deprived the country of a stable currency. To guard against further land speculation, President Jackson issued the Specie Circular, which required the payment for public lands to be in gold or silver. This policy eventually resulted in diminishing the value of paper money. Prices of land, cotton and slaves spiraled downward in Alabama. Governor Clay responded to the economic crisis by calling a special session of the legislature, which enacted the Relief Act of 1837 to sanction the suspension of specie payments by the banks, suspend collection of debts and require the issuance of $5 million in bonds by the branch banks. These measures left the state bank with unmanageable indebtedness, which, along with the factors mentioned above, contributed to its eventual closure.[147]

The General Assembly and nine governors dealt with myriad other issues during the capital's stay in Tuscaloosa. Most notably, in 1839, the General Assembly passed a bill authorizing construction of the state's first penitentiary in Wetumpka. In 1844, it enacted legislation allowing the Montgomery & West Point Railroad and the Tennessee & Coosa Railroad to borrow money from the 2 percent fund. On the surface, this bill was not particularly noteworthy. In turn, however, this allowed Charles Pollard, principal owner of the Montgomery & West Point Railroad, to commence a venture with the Tennessee & Coosa Railroad to establish a rail route that threatened the only trade route between the Tennessee Valley and south Alabama, which ran through Tuscaloosa. Such legislation provided some indication of what was likely to come of Tuscaloosa's continuing viability as the state capital. Sentiment had begun building for the removal of the capital from Tuscaloosa as early as the mid-1830s. Losing the main branch of the state bank, the possibility of losing its status as having the sole trade route to south Alabama by way of the Huntsville Road, the fact that the Black Warrior River was navigable for only a portion of the year, a shift in the population southeastward as nine new counties were carved out of the Treaty of Cusetta and political power shifting from north Alabama to the Black Belt all but guaranteed that the capital would be removed from Tuscaloosa. Indeed, on January 24, 1845, the General Assembly passed a joint resolution proposing an amendment to the state constitution that would allow the relocation of state capital.[148]

Thomas Chalmers McCorvey's poem "The Old Capitol at Tuscaloosa" reflects on Tuscaloosa's twenty-year reign as the state's capital:

Proud stands the Capital on "Childress hill,"
Still nobly bowered in primeval oaks,
And hears the Warrior waters dash their foam
And thunder down the Appalachian rocks…
The mordant years defy. Beneath its dome
The deeply pious, democratic Murphy,
With Scotia's accent rich upon his tongue;
The gallant Gayle, who dared "Old Hickory's" frown;
The fearless Bagby, with every gift save thrift;
And many another leader, bold and true,
The buoyant steps of the adolescent state
Firm guided on the path to fair renown. . .

…'Twas here
The great-souled patriot-poet, Francis Key—
He who the starry banner sang to fame—
Brought words of balm to a defiant state…

The memories of the Capitol are one
With those who sleep in nearby "Greenwood" graves…[149]

In August 1845, the Alabama electorate voted overwhelmingly to approve the amendment allowing for the relocation of the seat of government. The legislature, pursuant to the constitution, had to again approve the amendment, which it did on January 21, 1846. The way was then open for towns and cities to make their pitches to become Alabama's fifth capital. In the meantime, the capital was to remain in Tuscaloosa until a new site was selected. On January 28, 1846, a joint session of the General Assembly met and, after sixteen ballots, chose Montgomery as the next capital over Tuscaloosa, Wetumpka, Mobile, Statesville, Selma, Marion and Huntsville. More and more attention would be paid to states' rights and the defense of slavery as the capital moved one last time to Montgomery, which still serves as Alabama's capital some 168 years later. For approximately three months in 1861, Montgomery also briefly served as the capital of the Confederate States of America before it was moved to Richmond, Virginia.[150]

Tuscaloosa's Post-Capital Years (1846–Present)

The loss of the capital was initially crushing to Tuscaloosa. Immediately before the removal of the capital in 1845, Tuscaloosa's population was 4,250. Five years later, in 1850, the population had been cut by more than half, to only 1,950. Much of this decline could be attributed to the loss of government employees and lobbyists, who left for Montgomery. Of course, with the loss of residents, business suffered and real estate values plunged. Also, as we have seen, just a few years before its loss of the capital, Tuscaloosa suffered another major setback when it was hit with a destructive tornado, which destroyed many of the town's original structures. Luckily, the capitol building was spared significant damage, losing only a few shingles from its roof. Tuscaloosa was not left in complete disarray, however, as the University of Alabama remained a strong presence in the Druid City. In January 1852, the state donated the abandoned capitol building and its grounds to the University of Alabama to be used for educational purposes. Several proposals were made about what to do with the building before the university board of trustees decided to lease the capitol to the recently established Baptist-affiliated Alabama Central Female College in the fall of 1857. In 1859, conditions improved further when construction was completed on the Alabama Insane Hospital (now known as Bryce Hospital), which had been established by the General Assembly in 1852.[151]

In hopes of resolving the disciplinary problems of the student body and in anticipation of a possible war with the North, on February 23, 1860, the Alabama General Assembly authorized the University of Alabama to create a military department and to place all students under a code of military discipline. President Landon C. Garland, who had advocated for a military academy since 1855, became superintendent of the Alabama Corps of Cadets when the school opened in 1860 as a military institution. It was not long before the stereotype of a rowdy and ungovernable student body had been eradicated. Unfortunately, by this time, the state had seceded and was at war, which instilled in many of the cadets a desire to leave school and volunteer for service in local units being formed throughout the state. President Garland was vehemently opposed to students leaving school, emphasizing that those who completed their studies and military training would be of greater value to the Confederacy. Also, he argued that cadets could come to the aid of Tuscaloosa in the event of a slave insurrection and could provide needed training to volunteer units throughout the state. Despite President

Garland's efforts, more and more students left the university prior to completion of their studies and training. Many students stayed just long enough to learn the basics of military service before leaving to join volunteer units in their home communities.[152]

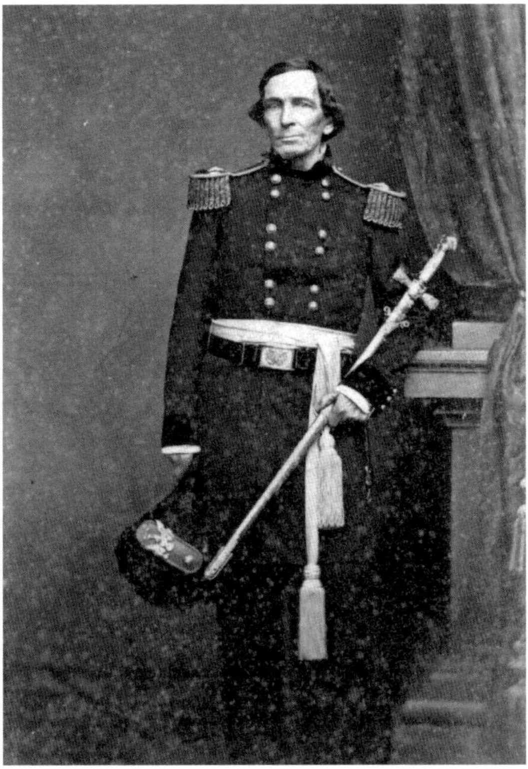

Garland C. Landon (1810–1895), third president of the University of Alabama, served as superintendent of the Alabama Corps of Cadets. *Courtesy Alabama Department of Archives and History.*

Despite the rapidity of many students' matriculation, the university nevertheless developed a reputation as an efficient training academy, making it a rich military target. With the hopes of a Confederate victory fading, President Garland was convinced that Federal forces would eventually attack the university. Indeed, in April 1865, in the closing days of the war, a detachment of General James H. Wilson's raiders under the command of General John T. Croxton were sent to destroy the "bridge, factories, mills, university (military school) and whatever else may be of benefit to the rebel cause." Members of Tuscaloosa's home guard, composed of old men and boys, unsuccessfully tried to fend off Croxton's troops. Greatly outnumbered, the home guard soldiers made a quick retreat after a very minor skirmish as the Federal troops came pouring over the bridge across the Black Warrior River. This allowed Croxton's troops to enter Tuscaloosa. Upon learning this news, President Garland called the Corps of Cadets into action. They soon encountered Federal forces when they got to the center of town and briefly engaged them in a short exchange of gunfire in which they killed three Union soldiers. However, when Garland realized how badly his Corps of Cadets was outnumbered, he ordered a retreat back to campus, where the cadets provisioned themselves for a march to safety in Marion, Alabama. Meanwhile, both Tuscaloosa and the campus of the University of Alabama were at the mercy of the invading Federal forces. Not much mercy was shown as the raiders destroyed a foundry, a saltpeter factory, a tannery, a Confederate hat factory and two large cotton warehouses. Although there was purportedly no widespread looting, a great number of horses and mules were confiscated, several stores were plundered and a number of valuables were stolen from Tuscaloosa residences.[153]

The most significant destruction occurred on the campus of the University of Alabama, where all but four structures were destroyed. While mills and factories along the riverfront were being burned, General Croxton dispatched Colonel Thomas M. Johnston of the Second Michigan Cavalry to the university with orders to burn it to the ground. When the Second Michigan Cavalry reached the campus on the morning of April 4, 1865, André DeLoffre, a professor of modern language and the school's librarian, pleaded with its commanding officer not to burn the Rotunda, asserting that it housed one of the finest libraries in the South. Colonel Thomas was sympathetic with this appeal and sent a messenger to General Croxton seeking permission to save the library from destruction. Croxton declined this request, stating that he had no discretion in the matter since his orders required him to destroy all public buildings. Legend has it that before the library was set on fire, someone—presumably DeLoffre—was allowed to retrieve one book. The legend continues that the book chosen to be retrieved was an English translation of the Koran, entitled *The Koran: Commonly Called the Alcoran of Mohammed*. Louisa Frances Garland, wife of President Garland, fared better than DeLoffre, as she was able to spare the president's mansion from destruction by chiding Union soldiers into putting out the fire that they had already started within the house. Also avoiding destruction was the Gorgas House, which was a campus hotel at the time; the observatory; and a guardhouse (now known as Jason's Shrine). All of these structures have survived to this day.[154]

Tuscaloosa and the University of Alabama suffered like the rest of the South with the commencement of Reconstruction. The university closed when the Corps of Cadets of 1864–65 did not reconvene after fleeing from the campus on April 4, 1865. Things began looking up again when the university reopened in 1871. In 1872, the university got a boost in the arm with the founding of its school of law by Henderson Middleton Somerville. The Alabama Insane Hospital, which had opened just before the Civil War, was left intact by Wilson's Raiders. Also of great benefit to Tuscaloosa was the construction a new system of locks and dams on the Black Warrior River, constructed by the U.S. Army Corps of Engineers in the 1890s, which

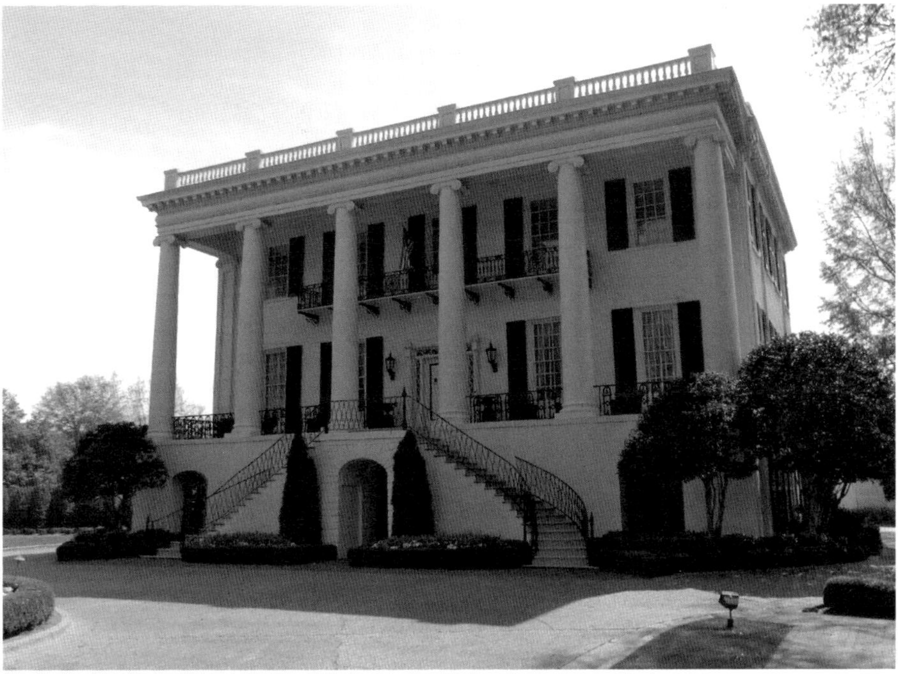

The president's mansion at the University of Alabama as it looks today. *Taken by author.*

provided the city with an improved outlet to Mobile's seaport. While all these were positive steps for Tuscaloosa, it would take until the commencement of the twentieth century for the city to fully recover from the physical and economic devastation that had been dealt it by war. By that time, it had become one of the state's major population centers, and the university's growth had made it the state's education center.[155]

Tuscaloosa and Alabama, however, would change forever as a result of events occurring in the 1950s and the early 1960s. Monumental change was on the horizon in February 1956, when an African American woman by the name of Autherine Lucy attempted to enroll as a student at the then all-white University of Alabama. She had been accepted for admittance in 1952, but when administrators discovered her race, they refused to enroll her. This led to a three-year legal battle that ended on June 29, 1955, when U.S. District Court judge Hobart Grooms entered an order prohibiting university officials from denying Lucy's admission. Accordingly, she enrolled on February 1, 1956, but her stay would be very short, as her presence set off violent demonstrations. On the third day of attending classes, she was surrounded by a hostile mob from which she escaped and was taken away lying down in the back seat of a patrol car. The board of trustees then voted to exclude Lucy from the university, supposedly for her own safety. It later permanently expelled her after her attorney filed a complaint on her behalf alleging that the university had conspired with the mob to preclude her from attending classes. Although the complaint was withdrawn, the expulsion remained in effect. It would be seven more years before the university was successfully integrated. On June 11, 1963, two African Americans, Vivian Malone and James Hood, were admitted as students after the infamous "stand in the schoolhouse door" staged by Governor George C. Wallace. The governor refused to allow the students to enter Foster Auditorium to register and read a prepared statement denouncing the federal government. When President Kennedy federalized the Alabama National Guard thereafter, Governor Wallace made a short final statement and stepped aside so that Malone and Hood could enter to register and become the first African Americans to attend the University of Alabama. Significantly, since that time, the numbers of African Americans enrolled at the university have grown to make up 12 percent of the student body.[156]

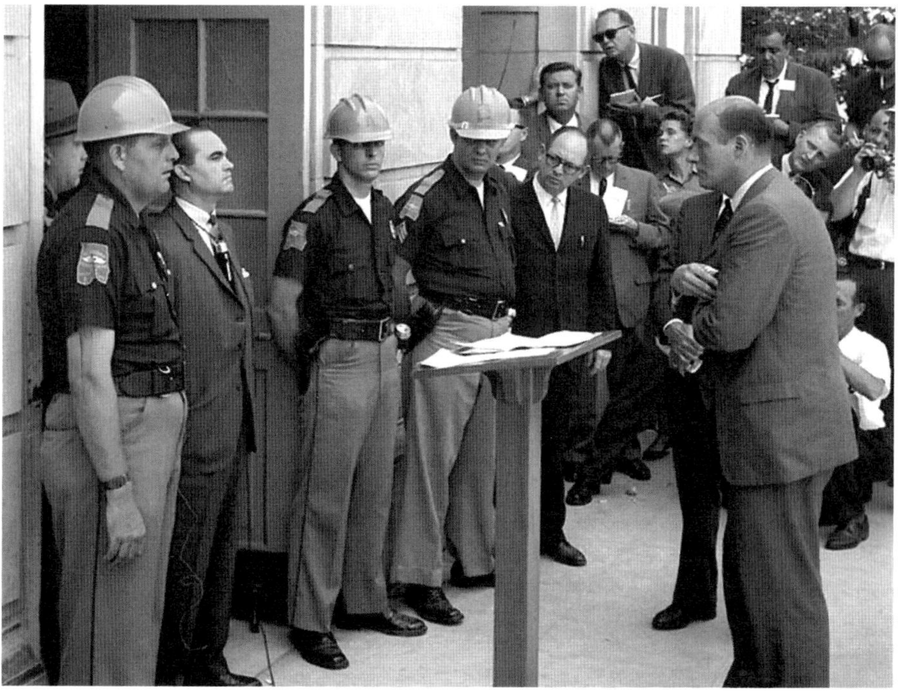

Governor George Wallace standing in the "schoolhouse door" in June 1963 in an effort to deny admission to two African American students in June 1963. *Released to public domain by* U.S. News & World Report *magazine.*

Today, Tuscaloosa is one of Alabama's premier cities and, as a beneficiary of a global economy, is now the hub for West Alabama industry and commerce. In the later part of the twentieth century, Tuscaloosa attracted such large manufacturing firms as Michelin and JVC before being chosen by Mercedes-Benz in 1993 to launch Alabama into the automotive industry. Although these firms contribute greatly to Tuscaloosa's economy, the University of Alabama undoubtedly remains the city's economic and cultural leader. In the most recent decade, the university has been consistently ranked among the top fifty public state universities in the *U.S. News & World Report*'s annual college rankings. In 2013, it reached a record enrollment of 34,852, a far cry from the first class in 1831, which consisted of 52 young men. The university's School of Law was ranked twenty-first among all law schools in the nation in the spring of 2013. The university has also excelled in athletics over the years, producing numerous championship teams in several different sports. Known particularly for its football prowess, it has won fifteen national championships under Coach Wallace Wade, Coach Frank Thomas, Coach Gene Stallings, Coach Paul William "Bear" Bryant and Coach Nick Saban.

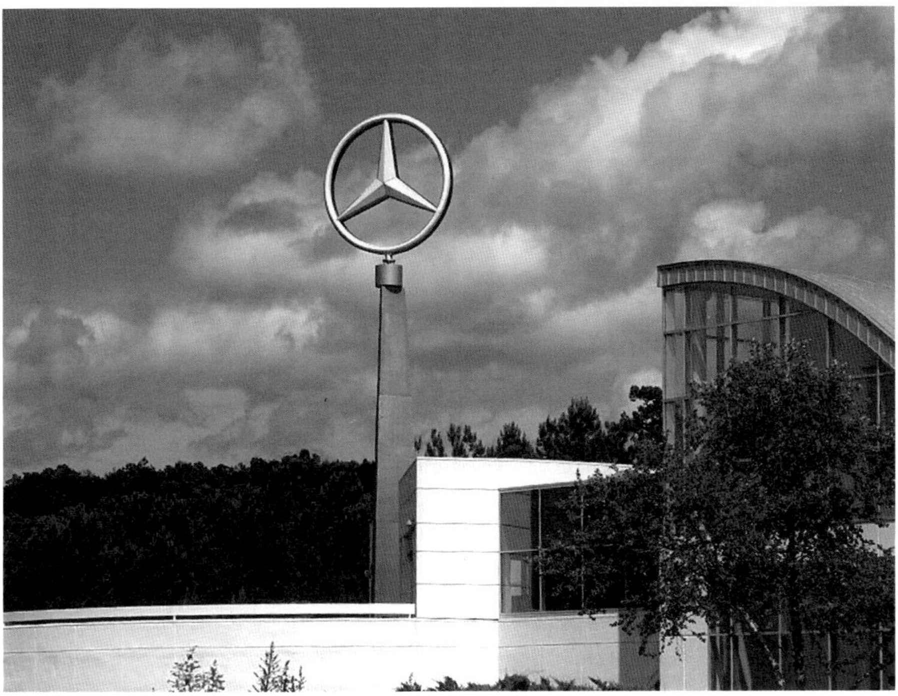

A Mercedes-Benz plant is evidence of Tuscaloosa's successful participation in today's global market. *Library of Congress.*

National championships in other sports have been won by the women's gymnastics team six times, the men's golf team twice and one each by the women's golf team and the women's softball team.[157]

In 2011, Tuscaloosa was named the "Most Livable City in America" by the U.S. Conference of Mayors. Unfortunately, also in 2011, Tuscaloosa was hit by a powerful EF4 tornado that destroyed entire neighborhoods and tragically resulted in forty-four fatalities, including six students at the University of Alabama. Tuscaloosa has endured much through the years—the 1840s tornado that destroyed many of the town's original structures, the loss of the state capital to Montgomery, the burning of its industries and the University of Alabama by Yankee soldiers during the closing days of the Civil War, the negativity and racial tensions created by Governor George Wallace's stand in the schoolhouse door and the devastating tornado that struck the city on April 27, 2011. Its citizens, however, can be only encouraged by how their town has always seemed to bounce back from adversity even stronger and more determined than ever before.

NOTES

CHAPTER 1

1. Brantley, *Three Capitals*; Lewis, "Old St. Stephens."
2. Mast, "Fort Tombeckbe"; Hannings, *Forts of the United States*, 11–12.; Brantley, *Three Capitals*, 1–3.
3. Hannings, *Forts of the United* States, 11–12; Brantley, *Three Capitals*, 2–4; Lewis, "Old St. Stephens"; Pate, "Fort of the Confederation," 171.
4. Pate, "Fort of the Confederation," 184–86; Lewis, "Old St. Stephens"; Hannings, *Forts of the United States*, 11–12; Holmes, "Notes on the Spanish Fort San Esteban De Tombecbe," 289; Brantley, *Three Capitals*, 4.
5. Hamilton, "St. Stephens," 230; Brantley, *Three Capitals*, 6; Joseph Chambers to Governor W.C.C. Claiborne; "History of Old St. Stephens"; Pate, *Reminiscences of George Strothers Gaines*, 154.
6. Briceland, "Ephraim Kirby," 83; "An Act Providing for the Disposal of Land South of Tennessee," 1937, 192–205; Lewis, *Clearing the Thickets*, 60.
7. Lewis, *Clearing the Thickets*, 61–62; Ephraim Kirby to William Simpson, March 25, 1804; Briceland, "Ephraim Kirby," 97–98.
8. Briceland, "Ephraim Kirby," 110–11; Lewis, *Clearing the Thickets*, 63–65. The term "filibusterers" refers to private adventurers who take part in military actions against foreign nations.
9. Pruitt, *Taming Alabama*, 1–13; Lewis, *Clearing the Thickets*, 63–67.
10. Edwin Lewis was an early settler of the Mississippi Territory who was frequently at odds with local federal officials with regard to conflicting land

titles, as well as his filibustering activities against the Spanish in Mobile. James Madison from Edwin Lewis, November 21, 1810 (Abstract).

11. Brantley, *Three Capitals*, 7; *Toulmin's Mississippi Territory Statutes*; *Turner's Digest of the Laws of the Mississippi Territory*, 106; Hamilton, "American St. Stephens," 83.

12. Carter, *Territorial Papers*, vol. 6, 618–22; Lewis, *Clearing the Thickets*, 65–66.

13. *Old St. Stephens: Historical Records Survey*, 1997, 74, 76–77, 86; 1816 Treaty of St. Stephens, October 24, 1816; Proclamation, December 30, 1816, 137. On September 5, 1813, Jesse Griffin wrote to his parents from St. Stephens indicating that he and his family had traveled fifty miles from his home, dodging a rampage of violence committed by Creek warriors against settlers in an area covering some one hundred miles of frontier in southwest Alabama. He believed that a minimum of "four hundred souls" had been slain by these warriors within a period of five days. Although their lives were spared, Jesse lamented that he had lost his crop of corn, his horses and other stock, as well as a good part of their household furniture. Letter from Jesse Griffin to his parents, September 5, 1813.

14. Dow and Dow, *History of Cosmopolite*, 101, 220; *Old St. Stephens*, 1997, 93, quoting A.P. Hayne to Major General Andrew Jackson, Town of St. Stephens, November 27, 1816; *Toulmin's Digest*, 108; Matte, *History of Washington County*, 50. McIntosh Bluff had been the county seat when Harry Toulmin arrived in 1804 to serve as a federal judge, but Toulmin moved it to Wakefield. However, county lines changed in 1809, and Wakefield became part of Baldwin County.

15. *Toulmin's Digest*, 540–41.

16. Brantley, *Three Capitals*, 9; *Toulmin's Digest*, 542–43.

17. Brantley, *Three Capitals*, 41; *Senate Journal*, February 3, 1818, 22; Lewis, *Clearing the Thickets*, 289; Matte, *History of Washington County*, 59; Ellison, *History and Bibliography of Alabama Newspapers*, 157.

18. John Pomery, unpublished sketch of Henry Hitchcock, circa 1867, and Hitchcock to Pomery, April 12, 1817, both quoted in Bigham, "From the Green Mountains to the Tombigbee," 213–15.

19. *Alabama Republican*, September 30, 1817, as quoted in Griffith, *Alabama*, 178–79.

20. *Act Establishing the Alabama Territory* in Carter, *Territorial Papers*, vol. 18, 53–57; Brantley, *Three Capitals*, 23; Lewis, *Clearing the Thickets*, 113.

21. Abernethy, *Formative Period in Alabama*, 50; Lewis, *Clearing the Thickets*, 114–16; *Journal of the Legislative Council of the Alabama Territory at the First Session*, 1–12.

22. *Old St. Stephens*, 46–47; *Acts Passed at the First Session*, 22–24, hereafter cited as *Ala. Acts*, 1 Sess.
23. *Ala. Acts*, 1 Sess. 1818, 50–52; Nelms, "Early Days with the Alabama River Steamboats," 13–14; Ward, *Tombigbee River Steamboats*, 23; *Old St. Stephens*, 55, citing the *Halcyon and Tombeckbe Public Advertiser*, May 15, 1820.
24. *Ala. Acts*, 1 Sess. 1818, 62–63; Bailey, "Israel Pickens, People's Politician," 83–84; Lewis, *Clearing the Thickets*, 169; Welsh, "Reminisces of Old St. Stephens," 221.
25. *Ala. Acts*, 1 Sess. 1818, 3–116. The repeal of the usury law limiting interest rates was very controversial, so much so that it, too, became the subject of repeal by the first legislature of the State of Alabama. Lewis, *Clearing the Thickets*, 118.
26. J.S.W. Parkin to Jno. R. Parker, May 15, 1819; Matte, *History of Washington County*, 59; *Old St. Stephens* 19.
27. *Old St. Stephens*, 17–18.
28. Ibid., 17–20, 45–64; Brantley, *Three Capitals*, 40–41. It should be noted that some of these businesses were not opened until a year or two after the capital was moved to Huntsville, but they were all in existence when St. Stephens was still a vibrant town.
29. *Old St. Stephens*, 17, 19, 47; Fairly, "Lost Capitals of St. Stephens and Cahawba," 22; Brantley, *Three Capitals*, 41; Matte, *History of Washington County*, 59.
30. *Old St. Stephens*, 17–18, 52–62; "Alabama's Supreme Court Justices, Reuben Saffold"; Lewis, "Henry Hitchcock"; "Francis Strother Lyon"; "William Crawford, 1784–1849." While serving as federal district attorney, Crawford prosecuted postmaster R.H. Gilmer for theft of money from the U.S. mail. Crawford barely escaped death when Gilmer waylaid him and shot him with a shotgun, some twenty of its balls entering his body. Gilmer was pursued and committed suicide in the presence of his would-be captors. Crawford recovered completely and continued his distinctive career. Welsh, "Reminiscences of Old St. Stephens," 225. James Caller described Gilmer as one of the most "frivolous, vicious, and abandoned characters in the country." Lewis, *Clearing the Thickets*, 66.
31. Brantley, *Three Capitals*, 41; Robertson, "Lewis Sewell"; Lewis, *Clearing the Thickets*, 290.
32. Welsh, "Reminiscences of Old St. Stephens," 210, n. 4; *Old St. Stephens*, 54, 57.
33. *Old St. Stephens*, 18; see generally Jeffrey C. Benton, *Respectable and Disreputable: Leisure Time in Antebellum Montgomery* (Montgomery, AL: New South Books, 2013).

34. *Old St. Stephens*, 50, 64; Matte, *History of Washington County*, 59; *Halcyon and Tombeckbe Public Advertiser*, July 6, 1822.
35. *Old St. Stephens*, 43, 58–59; Stockham, "Misunderstood Lorenzo Dow," 20.
36. *Ala. Acts*, 2 Sess. 1818, 10; *Acts Passed at the Second Session of the First General Assembly*, 38; *Ala. Acts*, 2 Sess. 1818, 3–4, 49; Lewis, *Clearing the Thickets*, 120.
37. *Ala. Acts*, 1 Sess. 1818, 94–95; *Ala. Acts*, 2 Sess. 1818, 49; Lewis, *Clearing the Thickets*, 120–21.
38. *Old St. Stephens*, 63, quoting the March 30, 1822 issue of the *Halcyon and Tombeckbe Public Advertiser*; Welsh, "Reminiscences of Old St. Stephens," 210; Lewis, "Old St. Stephens"; Sledge, "St. Stephens Historical Overview."
39. "Archaeology at Old St. Stephens"; "Volunteers Unearth Alabama's Past at Old St. Stephens."
40. Sarah Kershaw, "Amid the Ghosts of Alabama," *New York Times*, April 18, 2008.

Chapter 2

41. *Statutes of Mississippi Territory*, 1816, 98, 177–78, cited in Betts, *Early History of Huntsville*, 14, 19–21, 14–15.
42. *Treaty with the Chickasaw*; *Treaty with the Cherokee*; Luttrell, *Historical Markers of Huntsville*, 3; Taylor, "Early History of Madison County," 110; Dupre, *Transforming the Cotton Frontier*, 19; Betts, *Early History of Huntsville*, 28; Anne Royall to Mathew Dunbar, Huntsville, January 1, 1818 in Royall, *Letters from Alabama*, 43–44.
43. Dupre, *Transforming the Cotton Frontier*, 26; Luttrell, *Markers of Madison County*, 3; Lewis, *Clearing the Thickets*, 108.
44. Lewis, *Clearing the Thickets*, 109; Dupre, *Transforming the Cotton Frontier*, 37; *Statutes of Mississippi Territory*, 1816, 100, cited in Betts, *Early History of Huntsville*, 26; see also Eleanor Newman Hutchins, "Why Twickenham?: A Speculation on the Vision of the Founders," *Huntsville Historical Review* 15 (Spring/Fall 1985): 10 for a discussion of the naming of the town "Twickenham" and the reversal of this decision by the legislature.
45. Dupre, *Transforming the Cotton Frontier*, 38; Anne Royall to Mathew Dunbar, Huntsville, January 1, 1818, in Royall, *Letters from Alabama*, 43–44.
46. Mathews, *Why Public Schools?*, 50–53; Anne Royall to Mathew Dunbar, Huntsville, January 1, 1818, in Royall, *Letters from Alabama*, 44; O.C.

Skipper, "Huntsville's Green Academy," 17; Fisk, *Civilization Comes to the Big Spring*, 3; Rohr, "The Early Years"; "Green Bottom Inn"; Sulzby, *Historic Alabama Hotels and Resorts*, 147.

47. Betts, *Early History of Huntsville*, 28; Dupre, *Transforming the Cotton Frontier*, 38–39; Byers, "Two Hundred Years," 52.

48. Betts, *Early History of Huntsville*, 32; *Statutes of Mississippi Territory*, 1816, 455; Jones, "First National Bank," 5; Lewis, *Clearing the Thickets*, 118–19.

49. Betts, *Early History of Huntsville*, 33–34.

50. Abernethy, *Formative Period*, 66–68; Dupre, *Transforming the Cotton Frontier*, 45; Lewis, *Clearing the Thickets*, 123–24.

51. Betts, *Early History of Huntsville*, 34; Taylor, "Early History of Madison County," 166; Byers, "Two Hundred Years," 49.; Fisk, "Williams Street Area in the Early 1800s," 18–26; "Helion Lodge"; *Halcyon and Tombeckbe Public Advertiser*, December 25, 1819.

52. *Act to Enable the People of Alabama Territory to form a Constitution* [passed March 2, 1819].

53. Thomas McAdory Owen, ed. "The Visit of President James Monroe to Alabama Territory, June 1, 1819," *Transactions of the Alabama Historical Society* 3 (1898–99): 128–30 (based on an article published in the St. Stephens *Halcyon and* the *Tombeckbe Public Advertiser*, June 28, 1819, reprinted from Huntsville's *Alabama Republican*, Saturday, June 5, 1819); Dupre, *Transforming the Cotton Frontier*, 47; Brantley, *Three Capitals*, 43 (quoting from the June 26, 1819 issue of Huntsville's *Alabama Republican*).

54. Brannon, "Interesting Characters of the Constitutional Convention," 388–89; McMillan, "Constitution of 1819," 74–77; "Alabama Constitution Village." All of these structures have been rebuilt on their original sites and now are a part of the Alabama Constitution Village, which is currently one of three museums funded by the Alabama Constitution Village Foundation (see http://www.earlyworks.com/earlyworks-foundation/); Fisk, "Mapping 1819 Huntsville in Retrospect," 21–23 (from a talk given by Sarah Fluff Fisk at the opening of Constitution Hall Park, now Alabama Constitution Village, on May 1, 1982).

55. McMillan, *Constitutional Development in Alabama*, 32–33; "Journal of the Constitution," 131.

56. Lewis, *Clearing the Thickets*, 135–36.

57. McMillan, *Constitutional Development in Alabama*, 36–37; *Alabama Constitution of 1819*, Art. IV, Secs. 14, 23; Art. V, Secs. 12–13.; Abernethy, *Formative Period*, 55–57.

58. Lewis, *Clearing the Thickets*, 138; *Alabama Constitution of 1819*, Art. III, Sec. 29.
59. McMillan, *Constitutional Development in Alabama*, 45; *Official Journal of the Constitutional Convention of 1819*, 39–40.
60. Lewis, *Clearing the Thickets*, 144; Atkins, "First Legislative Session," 31.
61. *Alabama House Journal (1819)*, 8–16; Atkins, "The First Legislative Session," 31; *Acts of the General Assembly of the State of Alabama*, 1819, 136; Brantley, *Three Capitals*, 49–52.
62. *Ala. Acts*, 1819, 3–150; Atkins, "First Legislative Session," 31–44; Lewis, *Clearing the Thickets*, 150–59.
63. Lewis, *Clearing the Thickets*, 159.
64. Rohr, "News from Huntsville," 3; Huntsville's *Alabama Republican*, February 5, 1820; Betts, *Early History of Huntsville*, 45–46.
65. Royall, *Letters from Alabama*, 152.
66. Betts, *Early History of Huntsville*, 46–47, 71; Schmidt, "Huntsville"; Lewis, *Clearing the Thickets*, 208.
67. Betts, *Early History of Huntsville*, 49, 75.
68. Bounds, "Disaffection in Madison County," 3.
69. Schmidt, "Huntsville"; Betts, *Early History of Huntsville*, 96–97; *The War of the Rebellion: A Compilation of the Official Records of the Union and Confederate Armies*, vol. X, eHistory at Ohio State University, http://ehistory.osu.edu/osu/sources/recordView.cfm?Content=011/0111 (accessed January 24, 2014); Deborah Storer, "Civil War: 150th Anniversary of the Union Occupation of Huntsville," *Huntsville Times* (AL.Com), http://blog.al.com/breaking/2012/04/the_civil_war_union_occupation.html (accessed January 24, 2014); Martha B. Gabel, "General O.M. Mitchel's Occupation of Huntsville," *Huntsville Historical Review* 1 (July 1971): 12.
70. Schmidt, "Huntsville"; Lewis, "Madison County."
71. Ibid.
72. "U.S. Space and Rocket Center," http://rocketcenter.com/.

Chapter 3

73. Keith, *Old Cahaba*, 4–7; "The Cahaba Foundation"; Lewis, *Clearing the Thickets*, 14.
74. Keith, *Old Cahaba*, 7–8; Lewis, "Cahaba." In 1540, De Soto's conquistadores were involved in a massive battle at the town of Mabila wherein as many as five thousand Native Americans were killed. There

has been much debate about where Mabila was located, but no consensus has yet been reached among scholars who have studied the question. Old Cahawba is a possible site, although no evidence has yet been found to support that theory. See Vernon J. Knight, ed., *The Search for Mabila: The Decisive Battle Between Hernando de Soto and Chief Tascalusa* (Tuscaloosa: University of Alabama Press, 2009).

75. Keith, *Old Cahaba*, 10; Lewis, *Clearing the Thickets*, 105.

76. *Ala. House Journal*, 2 Sess. 1818, 15.

77. *Ala. Acts*, 2 Sess. 1818, 46–49.

78. Ibid., 47; *Ala. House Journal*, 1819, 8–16; Hobbs, "History of Early Cahaba," 164–65; Walter M. Jackson, *The Story of Selma* (Birmingham, AL: Birmingham Printing Company, 1954), 6–7; Brantley, *Three Capitals*, 63.

79. Brantley, *Three Capitals*, 63–67 (building specifications quoted from St. Stephens's *Halcyon and Tombeckbe Public Advertiser*, April 5, 1819); Scott, "Cahaba," 15.

80. *Ala. Senate* Journal, 1 Sess. 1819, 16; Neville, *Glance at Old Cahawba*.

81. *Ala. Acts*, 1820, 33; *Minor's Reports*, 1–9; Meador, "Supreme Court of Alabama," 900–6.

82. Webb and Armbrester, "William Wyatt Bibb, 1819–1820, and Thomas Bibb, 1820–21," *Alabama Governors*, 15–17; Brantley, *Three Capitals*, 71–73; *Ala. Senate Journal*, 1820, 18–19; *Ala. Acts*, 1820, 63. On August 16, 1820, a large contingent met at Mrs. Campbell's Hotel to form a procession to the "academy," where Governor Bibb was eulogized. The order of procession was a follows: first Cahawba Guards, second citizens, third students of the academy, fourth physicians, fifth lawyers, sixth executive and state officers, seventh town council and eighth orator and clergy. *Alabama Watchman*, August 18, 1820.

83. *Ala. Const., 1819*, Art. IV, Sec. 18; *Journal of the Senate at the Second Session*, 10–11; *Ala. House Journal*, 1820, 121; *Ala. Acts*, 1820, 112.

84. Hobbs, "History of Early Cahaba," 168; *Alabama Watchman*, September 29, 1820. In an advertisement in the *Alabama Watchman*, numerous items were listed for sale, including lard, coffee, fresh flour, chocolate, molasses, wine, cognac, brandy, New England rum, gin, whiskey, silk handkerchiefs, silk, linens, silk and cotton hose, hammers, saws, files, knives, forks, spoons, plates, dishes, cups, saucers, hats, shoes, saddles, guns, powder and window sashes, to name just a few.

85. Hobbs, "History of Early Cahaba," 168; Brewer, *Alabama*; *Ala. Senate Journal*, 1823, 138; Fry, *Memories of Old Cahaba*, 12; *Alabama Watchman*, August 18 and 25, 1820.

86. Keith, *Old Cahaba*, 14; Fry, *Memories of Old Cahaba*, 13, 19.
87. Hobbs, "History of Early Cahaba," 176; *Cahawba Gazette*, January 7, 1826; Bangs, *History of the Methodist Episcopal Church*, 191.
88. Hobbs, "History of Early Cahaba," 169; *Alabama Watchman*, December 30, 1820; Owen, *Bibliography of Alabama*, 955–56 (from the Annual Report of the American Historical Association for 1897).
89. Hobbs, "History of Early Cahaba," 171; Nelms, "Early Days with the Alabama River Steamboats," 13–14; Fairly, "Lost Capitals of St. Stephens and Cahaba," 26. It is believed that the steamboat *Alabama*, constructed by the St. Stephens Steamboat Company, was the first steamboat to ply Alabama's waters when it steamed downstream from St. Stephens to Mobile in 1818. However, it was unable to generate enough power to make it back upriver and thus did not earn the distinction that had been garnered by the *Tensas* and *Harriet* steamboats.
90. The editor of Cahaba's *Intelligencer*, William B. Allen, jumped into the fray and tried to put Cahaba in the best light when he reported on June 21, 1823: "The town was never more healthy than at present—no death has happened here (with the exception of one which was occasioned by the running away of a horse and carriage) in more than seven months that we can recollect." Fairly, "Lost Capitals of St. Stephens and Cahawba," 26–28; Hobbs, "History of Early Cahaba," 170–71.
91. Lewis, *Clearing the Thickets*, 164–67; *Ala. Senate Journal*, Called Sess., 1821, 4–9.
92. Bailey, "Israel Pickens," 83–85; Thornton, *Politics and Power*, 16.
93. *Ala. House Journal*, 1821, 40–43, 58–64; Abernethy, *Formative Period*, 114–15; Bailey, "Israel Pickens," 87; Brantley, *Three Capitals*, 102–05; Moore, *History of Alabama*, 36–38; *Ala. Acts*, 1820), 20–27; *Ala. House Journal*, 1821, 227–33.
94. Bailey, "Israel Pickens," 93; Lewis, *Clearing the Thickets*, 178–79.
95. Bridges, "Nation's Guest," 8–17; McWilliams, "Marquis and the Myth," 137–39. It should be noted that there are a few discrepancies in the reporting of the exact itinerary of Lafayette, but for the most part, historians are consistent about the major events of Lafayette's tour.
96. Bridges, "Nation's Guest," 16; Scott, "Cahaba," 16.
97. Lowry, "Lafayette's Visit to Georgia and Alabama," 38–39; Fry, *Memories of Old Cahaba*, 25; McWilliams, "Marquis and the Myth," 143–44.
98. Bridges, "Nation's Guest," 16–17; Scott, "Cahaba," 16; Fry, "Memories of Old Cahaba," 25. According to Anna Gayle Fry, for years, the Bell Tavern had been the "favorite stopping place of the celebrated lawyers

when they visited the capital or attended court, and for the politicians and wealthy planters who gathered at this gay little metropolis on their way to Mobile." She continued, "Here they would spend days, 'waiting for the boat,' and passing the time in playing billiards or a gentlemanly game of poker, where the stakes nightly went far into the thousands, and valuable slaves frequently changed masters to satisfy a 'debt of honor.'"

99. Hobbs, "History of Early Cahaba," 173–74, quoting Griffith, *History of Alabama*, 162–64, being an excerpt from Auguste Levasseur's *Lafayette in America in 1824 and 1825 etc.* (Philadelphia, 1829), II, 75 ff.

100. Bridges, "Nation's Guest," 17, quoting from the *Cahaba Press*.

101. Lewis, *Clearing the Thickets*, 184–85; Bridges, "Nation's Guest," 17.

102. *Ala. Senate Journal*, 1825, 8–11; Bailey, "John Murphy," 22; *Ala. Acts*, 1825, 12.

103. *Ala. Acts*, 1825, 46–47, 74.

104. Lewis, *Clearing the Thickets*, 189.

105. Fry, *Memories of Old Cahaba*, 14, 16; Scott, "Cahaba," 17; Gosse, *Letters from Alabama*, 103; Jackson, *Rivers of History*, 68.

106. Fry, *Memories of Old Cahaba*, 15–16; Scott, "Cahaba," 18; Keith, *Old Cahaba*, 16.

107. Fry, *Memories of Old Cahaba*, 37–38; Keith, *Old Cahaba*, 16.

108. Fry, *Memories of Old Cahaba*, 37–38; Keith, *Old Cahaba*, 21; "Crocheron Columns" Historical Marker, Old Cahawba Archaeological Preserve, Orville, Alabama. (As we will see, the Crocheron Mansion played a significant role with regard to the aftermath of the Battle of Selma near the end of the Civil War.)

109. Fry, *Memories of Old Cahaba*, 19–20, 21, 32–33.

110. Keith, *Old Cahaba*, 26; Fry, *Memories of Old Cahaba*, 28, 32, 34–35. In this same block with the barbershop owned by the free African Americans were a grocery store, jewelry store, dry goods store, harness and saddle shop, post office, bakery and at least one saloon.

111. Owen, *History of Alabama*, 188; Scott, "Cahaba: Hallowed Ground," 18; Fry, Mem*ories of Old Cahaba*, 34.

112. Keith, *Old Cahawba*, 22–23; Scott, "Cahaba," 19.

113. Keith, *Old Cahawba*, 24; Scott, "Cahaba," 19. "Castle Morgan," the name given to Cahaba's prison by local citizens, was presumably in honor of cavalry general John Hunt Morgan, a native Alabamian who himself had recently escaped from the Ohio State Penitentiary. Fry, *Old Cahaba Memories*, 25.

114. Weerts, "Dinner Meeting Followed Battle."

115. Ambrose, "Remembering the Sultana"; Keith, *Old Cahaba*, 25; Scott, "Cahaba," 20. Some 520 people survived the accident, but it is not known how many had been prisoners at Castle Morgan. Of these, some 200 died later of injuries sustained in the accident.

116. Keith, *Old Cahaba*, 26–27. Clifton Kirkpatrick promoted diversified agriculture and at one time sat on the state's Board of Agriculture. An imposing figure at six-foot-four, he was known as the "Duke of Cahaba." Scott, "Cahaba," 20–21. For a more detailed look at Cahaba in the twentieth century, see Daniel J. Meador, *At Cahaba: From Civil War to Great Depression* (Brule, WI: Cable Publishing: 2000). Meador is the grandson of Clifton Kirkpatrick.

117. Fry, *Memories of Old Cahaba*, 69–70.

118. "The Cahaba Foundation."

119. Ibid.

Chapter 4

120. It should be noted that Dr. William Stokes Wyman, an early resident of Tuscaloosa, maintained that the name "Tuscaloosa" was common among the Choctaws and Creeks. Historian Mathew W. Clinton thus postulated that although it is not certain that Tuscaloosa was named for the great chief De Soto defeated in 1540, it is a pretty reasonable presumption that it would have been named for the best-known Indian of that name. Clinton, "De Soto First"; Blitz, *Moundville*, 61–71; Griffith, *Alabama*, 6. Tuscaloosa, which had large oak trees lining its downtown streets in its early days, is also sometimes referred to as the "Druid City"" after an ancient Celtic people who worshipped oaks. Lewis, "Tuscaloosa."

121. Clinton, *Tuscaloosa, Alabama*, 4–5, 35; Leftwich, "Colonel George Strothers Gaines," 447.

122. Griffith, *McIntosh and Weatherford*, 81–82; "Crawley Deposition," in John Spenser Bassett, ed. *Correspondence of Andrew Jackson* (Washington, D.C.: Carnegie Institution, 1926–1935), 1:225–26 n.1; Clinton, *Tuscaloosa Early Years*, 5–6; Pickett, *History of Alabama*, 515.

123. Pickett, *History of Alabama*, 552; Crockett, *Narrative*, 83–84.

124. Crockett, *Narrative*, 128; Clinton, *Tuscaloosa Early Years*, 10–11. There have been some who have concluded that Black Warrior's Town was located on the Mulberry Fork of the Black Warrior opposite the mouth of the Sipsey Fork in Walker County. As seen above, however,

Davy Crockett was very specific about the location of the town as being where Tuscaloosa was situated on the Falls of the Black Warrior. Some have postulated that the town was relocated to the Sipsey and Mulberry Forks after Colonel Coffee's troops destroyed the original town at the Falls of the Black Warrior. Wright, *Historic Indian Towns in Alabama*, 19–20.

125. Clinton, *Tuscaloosa Early Years*, 12–16.

126. Within in a year, all of the Lincecums left the Tuscaloosa area for a site on the Tombigbee River near present-day Columbus, Mississippi. Thereafter, living among the Choctaws, Gideon Lincecum practiced medicine and traded with the Indians for quite a number of years before moving on with his family to Texas. There, "he became known as the 'frontier naturalist,' practicing herbal medicine and studying the plant life of Texas." "Autobiography of Gideon Lincecum" (excerpted from *Publications of the Mississippi Historical Society* 8 [1904]: 443–509); Clinton, *Tuscaloosa Early Years*, 29; *Niles Weekly Register*, February 28, 1818, 15.

127. *Ala. Acts*, 1 Sess. 1818, 19; *Ala. Acts*, 1819, 106–08

128. Clinton, *Tuscaloosa Early Years*, 43–55; Robinson, "Newtown"; Slowe, "Looking Back."

129. Clinton, *Tuscaloosa Early Years*, 16–24.

130. Ibid., 31–32 (quoting from letters written by William H. Ely to his wife and the asylum back in Connecticut between early 1820 and the late summer of 1821). In one letter, he made it clear that he wished to be done with Alabama and "to return to my dear family & to a civilized and moral World." See William Ely to Clarissa Ely (April 20, 1820) and William Ely to Clarissa Ely (June 2, 1821), William Ely Letters.

131. McKenzie, "Newspapers and Newspaper Men," 187, 190; Gray, "Frontier Journalism," 183, 186; Ward, *Tombigbee River Steamboats*, 25–26; Clinton, "Steamboat Cotton Plant and the Salt Works"; Clinton, *Tuscaloosa Early Years*, 16–17, 36; "The University Club."

132. Clinton, *Tuscaloosa Early Years*, 38–41.

133. *Ala. Senate Journal*, 1825, 19, 31; Lewis, *Clearing the Thickets*, 187–88.

134. Mellown, "Alabama's Fourth Capital," 259–61; *Ala. House Journal*, 1826, 114; *Ala. Senate Journal*, 1827, 69, 109; *Ala. Senate Journal*, 1826, 137–38; Clinton, *Tuscaloosa Early Years*, 61–62.

135. *Ala. Senate Journal*, 1826, 111; Mellown, "Alabama's Fourth Capital," 263–65; *Ala. Senate Journal*, 1827, 46, 52, 66.

136. Mellown, "Alabama's Fourth Capital," 263–64; *Ala. Senate Journal*, 1827, 66.

137. Mellown, "Alabama's Fourth Capital," 264–67. During the cornerstone-laying festivities in 1827, a cannon burst into many pieces upon its ceremonious firing. These pieces were gathered up and later put into the walls of the capitol. *Ala. Senate Journal*, 1827, 66.
138. Clinton, *Tuscaloosa*, 63; Mellown, "Alabama's Fourth Capital," 274–75; *Ala. Senate Journal*, 1829, 7; Lewis, *Clearing the Thickets*, 196–97.
139. "Historical Account," 169a–170a.
140. Wolfe, *University of Alabama*, 10–13.
141. Sellers, *History of the University of Alabama*, 55–65; Sellers, "Student Life at the University of Alabama Before 1860," 272–74, 289–91; DuBose, *Sketches of Alabama History*, 155; *Ala. Acts*, 1836, 101–02.
142. Durham, *Southern Moderate in Radical Times*, 31–32; Smith, *Reminiscences of a Long Life*, 23, 214; Lewis, *Clearing the Thickets*, 261, 290–91. It should be noted that in the late 1840s, John Gorman Barr, a talented humorist, was part of a literary group headed by Professor Frederick A.P. Barnard, who later became president of Columbia University. This group also included William Russell Smith and Alexander Beaufort Meek and was referred to as Tuscaloosa's "Brilliant Galaxy of Young Men." Hoole, "John Gorman Barr," 83–116.
143. Tuscaloosa's *Alabama State Intelligencer*, January 19, 1831.
144. "Historical Account," 169a; Lewis, *Clearing the Thickets*, 200.
145. *Ala. House Journal*, 1826, 10–11; Rogers et al., *Alabama*, 84, 88; Brantley, *Banking in Alabama*, 30–33; Garrett, *Reminiscences of Public Men in Alabama*, 65–66; *Ala. Senate Journal*, 1837 Annual Sess., 44ff.
146. Wiggins, "John Gayle," in Webb and Armbrester, *Alabama Governors*, 32; *Treaty of Cusseta*, Art. 5; McCorvey, "Mission of Frances Scott Key," 141–53; Owsley, "Frances Scott Key's Mission to Alabama," 181–92; Brannon, "Creek Indian War," 156–158.
147. Rogers et al., *Alabama*, 138–39; Brantley, *Banking in Alabama*, 2:7; *Ala. Acts*, 1837, Called Sess., 9ff.
148. Lewis, *Clearing the Thickets*, 224–25.
149. McCorvey, *Alabama Historical Poems*, 15–17.
150. Simpson, "Alabama State Capital," 87–90; McMillan, "Selection of Montgomery as Alabama's Capital," 79–90.
151. Tuscaloosa historian Matthew Clinton indicates that "many people were of the opinion that the town had actually benefited from the removal because, with the capital, went many gamblers and other undesirable characters." Clinton, *Tuscaloosa*, 81, 87. The Alabama Central Female College remained as the capitol building's tenant until the old capitol was

destroyed by fire in 1923. Mellown, "Alabama's Fourth Capital," 279–81. Remnants of the old capitol building can be seen in Capitol Park at the western terminus of University Boulevard, just three blocks from downtown Tuscaloosa.

152. Wolfe, *University of Alabama*, 47–51.

153. Ibid., 54–59.

154. Ibid., 59–62; Taylor Holland, "Copy of Quran Only Book Saved from Union's 1865 Burning of UA," *Tuscaloosa News*, September 10, 2010, http://www.tuscaloosanews.com/article/20100910/NEWS/100909583?p=2&tc=pg&tc=ar (accessed April 29, 2014).

155. Wolfe, *University of Alabama*, 64, 75; Lewis, "Tuscaloosa."

156. Katz, "Autherine Lucy"; Dunn, "Stand in the School Door."

157. Lewis, "Tuscaloosa"; "University of Alabama: Did You Know"; "Official Home for the University of Alabama Athletics: Crimson Tide."

Selected Bibliography

Books

Abernethy, Thomas Perkins. *The Formative Period of Alabama, 1815–1828.* Montgomery: Alabama State Department of Archives and History (Historical and Patriotic Series no. 6), 1922. Reprint, Tuscaloosa: University of Alabama Press, 1995.

Bangs, Nathan. *A History of the Methodist Episcopal Church.* Vol. 3. New York: T. Mason and G. Lane, 1840.

Benton, Jeffrey C. *Respectable and Disreputable: Leisure Time in Antebellum Montgomery.* Montgomery, AL: New South Books, 2013.

Betts, Edward Chambers. *Early History of Huntsville, Alabama, 1804–1870.* 1909. Rev. ed. Montgomery, AL: Brown Printing Company, 1916.

Blitz, John H. *Moundville.* Tuscaloosa: University of Alabama Press, 2008.

Brantley, William H., Jr. *Banking in Alabama: 1816–1860.* Vol. 2. Birmingham, AL: Birmingham Printing Co., 1961.

———. *Three Capitals, A Book About the First Three Capitals of Alabama: St. Stephens, Huntsville, and Cahawba, 1818–1826.* 1947. Reprint, Tuscaloosa: University of Alabama Press, 1976.

Brewer, Willis. *Alabama, Her History, Resources, War Record, and Public Men from 1840 to 1872, 1872.* Reprint, Baltimore, MD: Genealogical Publishing Company, 2000.

Carter, Clarence E., ed. *Territorial Papers of the United States.* Vol. 5. Washington, D.C.: Government Printing Office, 1937.

Clinton, Matthew William. *Tuscaloosa, Alabama: Its Early Days, 1816, 1865*. Tuscaloosa, AL: Zonta Club, 1958.

Coleman, Ellison Rhoda. *History and Bibliography of Alabama Newspapers in the 19th Century*. Tuscaloosa: University of Alabama Press, 1954.

Crockett, David. *A Narrative of the Life of David Crocket of the State of Tennessee.* 1834. Reprint, Lincoln: University of Nebraska Press, 1987.

Dow, Reverend Larenzo, and Peggy Dow. *History of Cosmopolite: or, The Writings of Rev. Larenzo Dow: Containing His Experience and Travels, in Europe and America, Up to Near His Fiftieth Year. Also, His Polemic Writings. To Which Is Added, The "Journey of Life," by Peggy Dow, Revised and Corrected with Notes.* 8th ed. Cincinnati, OH: Applegate & Co., 1854.

DuBose, Joel C. *Sketches of Alabama History*. Philadelphia: Ellridge & Bro., 1901.

Dupre, Daniel S. *Transforming the Cotton Frontier: Madison County, Alabama, 1800–1840*. Baton Rouge: Louisiana State University Press, 1997.

Durham, David I. *A Southern Moderate in Radical Times: Henry Washington Hilliard, 1808–1892*. Baton Rouge: Louisiana State University Press, 2008.

Ellison, Rhoda Coleman. *History and Bibliography of Alabama Newspapers in the 19th Century.* Tuscaloosa: University of Alabama Press, 1954.

Fisk, Sarah Huff. *Civilization Comes to the Big Spring Huntsville Alabama 1823*. Huntsville, AL: Pinhook Publishing, 1970.

Fry, Anna M. Gayle. *Memories of Old Cahaba*. Nashville, TN: Publishing House for the Methodist Episcopal Church, South, 1908.

Garrett, William. *Reminiscences of Public Men in Alabama for Thirty Years.* Atlanta, GA: Plantation Publishing Company's Press, 1872.

Gosse, Phillip Henry. *Letters from Alabama, Chiefly Relating to Natural History*. Introduction by Harvey H. Jackson III. 1859. Reprint, Tuscaloosa: University of Alabama Press, 1993.

Griffith, Benjamin W., Jr. *McIntosh and Weatherford: Creek Indian Leaders*. Tuscaloosa: University of Alabama Press, 1988.

Griffith, Lucille. *Alabama: A Documentary History to 1900*. Rev. ed. Tuscaloosa: University of Alabama Press, 1972.

Hannings, Bud. *Forts of the United States: An Historical Dictionary, 16th through 19th Centuries.* Jefferson, NC: McFarland and Company, Inc., 2006.

Lewis, Herbert James. *Clearing the Thickets: A History of Antebellum Alabama*. New Orleans, LA: Quid Pro Books, 2013.

Luttrell, Frank Alex, III, ed. *Historical Markers of Huntsville, Alabama*. Huntsville, AL: Huntsville–Madison County Historical Society, 50th Anniversary, 1951–2001.

Mathews, Forest David. *Why Public Schools? Whose Public Schools? What Early Settlers Have to Tell Us*. Montgomery, AL: New South Books, 2002.

Matte, Jacqueline Anderson. *The History of Washington County, First County in Alabama.* Chatam, AL: Washington County Historical Society, 1982.

McCorvey, Thomas Chalmers. *Alabama Historical Poems.* Birmingham, AL: Birmingham Publishing Company, 1927 .

McMillan, Malcolm Cook. *Constitutional Development in Alabama, 1798–1901: A Study in Politics, the Negro, and Sectionalism.* Chapel Hill: University of North Carolina Press, 1955.

Meador, Daniel J. *At Cahaba: From Civil War to Great Depression.* Brule, WI: Cable Publishing, 2000.

Moore, Albert Burton. *History of Alabama.* 1934. Reprint, Tuscaloosa: Alabama Book Store, 1951.

Neville, Bert. *A Glance at Old Cahawba, Alabama's Early Capital.* Selma, AL: Coffee Printing Co., 1961.

Owen, Thomas McAdory. *A Bibliography of Alabama.* Washington, D.C.: Government Printing Office, 1898. [From the Annual Report of the American Historical Association for 1897.]

Pate, James P., ed.. *The Reminiscences of George Strothers Gaines: Pioneer and Statesman of Early Alabama and Mississippi, 1805–1843.* Tuscaloosa: University of Alabama Press, 1998.

Pickett, Albert James. *History of Alabama, and Incidentally of Georgia and Mississippi, From the Earliest Period.* 1851. Reprint, Birmingham, AL: Birmingham Book and Magazine Co., 1962.

Pruitt, Paul M., Jr. *Taming Alabama: Lawyers and Reformers, 1804–1929.* Tuscaloosa: University of Alabama Press, 2010.

Rogers, William Warren, et al. *Alabama: The History of a Deep South State.* Tuscaloosa: University of Alabama Press, 1994.

Royall, Anne. *Letters from Alabama on Various Subjects*. Washington, D.C., 1830.

Sellers, James B. *History of the University of Alabama.* Tuscaloosa: University of Alabama Press, 1953.

Smith, William Russell, Jr. *Reminiscences of a Long Life: Historical, Personal, and Literary.* Washington, D.C.: William R. Smith, 1889.

Sulzby, James Frederick. *Historic Alabama Hotels and Resorts.* 1960. Reprint, Tuscaloosa: University of Alabama Press, 1994.

Thornton, J. Mills, III. *Politics and Power in a Slave Society: Alabama 1800–1860.* Baton Rouge: Louisiana State University Press, 1978.

Ward, Rufus. *The Tombigbee River Steamboats: Rollodores, Dead Heads, and Side-Wheelers*. Charleston, SC: The History Press, 2010.

Webb, Samuel L., and Margaret E. Armbrester, eds. *Alabama Governors: A Political History of the State.* Tuscaloosa: University of Alabama Press, 2001.

Wolfe, Suzanne Rau. *The University of Alabama: A Pictorial History.* Tuscaloosa: University of Alabama Press, 1983.

Wright, Amos J., Jr. *Historic Indian Towns in Alabama, 1540–1838.* Tuscaloosa: University of Alabama Press, 2003.

Articles

Atkins, Leah. "The First Legislative Session: The General Assembly of Alabama, Huntsville, 1819." *Alabama Review* 23 (January 1970): 31.

Bailey, Hugh C. "Israel Pickens, People's Politician." *Alabama Review* 17 (April 1964): 83–84.

Bigham, Darrel E. "From the Green Mountains to the Tombigbee: Henry Hitchcock in Territorial Alabama, 1817–1819." *Alabama Review* 26 (July 1973): 213–15.

Bounds, Sarah Ethiline. "Disaffection in Madison County Before and During the Civil War." *Huntsville Historical Review* 4 (April 1974): 3.

Brannon, Peter A. "Creek Indian War, 1836–1837." *Alabama Historical Quarterly* 13 (1951): 156–58.

———. "Interesting Characters of the Constitutional Convention of Alabama of 1819." *Alabama Lawyer* 8 (October 1947): 388–89.

Briceland, Alan V. "Ephraim Kirby: Mr. Jefferson's Emissary on the Tombigbee-Mobile Frontier." *Alabama Review* 24 (April, 1971): 83.

Bridges, Edwin C. "The Nation's Guest: The Marquis de Lafayette's Tour of Alabama." *Alabama Heritage* (Fall 2011): 8–17.

Byers, David. "Two Hundred Years—The Big Spring and John Hunt." *Huntsville Historical Review* (Special Issue 2008).

Fisk, Sarah. "Mapping 1819 Huntsville in Retrospect." *Huntsville Historical Review* 33 (Winter/Spring 2008): 21–23.

———. "The Williams Street Area in the Early 1800s." *Huntsville Historical Review* 1 (January 1971): 18–26.

Gabel, Martha B. "General O.M. Mitchel's Occupation of Huntsville." *Huntsville Historical Review* 1 (July 1971): 12.

Gray, Daniel Savage. "Frontier Journalism: Newspapers in Antebellum Alabama." *Alabama Historical Quarterly* 37 (Fall 1975): 183, 186.

Hamilton, Peter J. "St. Stephens: Spanish Fort and American Town." *Transactions of the Alabama Historical Society* 3 (1898–99): 230.

Hobbs, Sam Earle. "History of Early Cahaba, Alabama's First State Capital." *Alabama Historical Quarterly* 31 (Fall/Winter 1969): 168.

Holmes, Jack D.L. "Notes on the Spanish Fort San Esteban De Tombecbe." *Alabama Review* 28 (October 1965): 289.

Hoole, W. Stanley. "John Gorman Barr: Forgotten Alabama Humorist." *Alabama Review* 4 (April 1951): 83–116.

Hutchins, Eleanor Newman. "Why Twickenham?: A Speculation on the Vision of the Founders." *Huntsville Historical Review* 15 (Spring/Fall 1985): 10.

Jones, Pat. "First National Bank." *Huntsville Historical Review* 5 (April–July 1975): 5.

"Journal of the Constitution, 1819, as Reported in Huntsville's *Alabama Republican*." *Alabama Historical Quarterly* 31 (Spring/Summer 1969): 131.

Leftwich, George J. "Colonel George Strothers Gaines and Other Pioneers in Mississippi Territory." *Publication of the Mississippi Historical Society* 1 (1916): 447.

Lowry, Lucille Cary. "Lafayette's Visit to Georgia and Alabama." *Alabama Historical Quarterly* 8 (Spring 1946): 38–39.

McCorvey, Thomas Chalmers. "The Mission of Frances Scott Key to Alabama in 1833." *Transactions to the Alabama Historical Society* 4 (1899–1903): 141–53.

McKenzie, Robert H. "Newspapers and Newspaper Men During Tuscaloosa's Capital Years, 1826–1846." *Alabama Historical Quarterly* 44 (Fall/Winter 1982): 187, 190.

McMillan, Malcolm Cook. "The Constitution of 1819: A Study of Constitution-Making on the Frontier." *Alabama Lawyer* 12 (January 1951): 7477.

———. "The Selection of Montgomery as Alabama's Capital." *Alabama Review* 1 (April 1948): 79–90.

McWilliams, Tennant S. "The Marquis and the Myth: Lafayette's Visit to Alabama, 1825." *Alabama Review* 22 (April 1969): 137–39.

Meador, Dean Daniel J. "The Supreme Court of Alabama: It's Cahaba Beginning, 1820–1825." *Alabama Law Review* 61 (2010): 900–6.

Mellown, Robert O. "Alabama's Fourth Capital: The Construction of the State House in Tuscaloosa." *Alabama Review* 40 (October 1987): 259–61.

Nelms, Jack N. "Early Days with the Alabama River Steamboats." *Alabama Review* 36 (January 1984): 13–14.

Owen, Thomas McAdory, ed. "The Visit of President James Monroe to Alabama Territory, June 1, 1819." *Transactions of the Alabama Historical Society* 3 (1898–99): 128–30.

Owsley, Frank A., Jr. "Frances Scott Key's Mission to Alabama in 1833." *Alabama Review* 23 (July 1970): 181–92.

Pate, James P. "The Fort of the Confederation: Spain on the Upper Tombigbee River." *Alabama Historical Quarterly* 44 (Fall/Winter 1982): 171.

Rohr, Nancy. "The News From Huntsville." *Huntsville Historical Review* 26 (January 1999): 3.

Scott, John. "Cahaba: Hallowed Ground." *Alabama Heritage* 99 (Winter 2011): 15.

Sellers, James B. "Student Life at the University of Alabama Before 1860." *Alabama Review* 4 (October 1949): 272–74.

Simpson, James B. "The Alabama State Capital: An Historical Sketch." *Alabama Historical Quarterly* 28 (Spring 1956): 87–90.

Skipper, O.C. "Huntsville's Green Academy: 1812–1862." *Huntsville Historical Review* 2 (October 1972): 17.

Taylor, Thomas Jones. "Early History of Madison County and, Incidentally of North Alabama." *Alabama Historical Quarterly* 1 (Spring 1930): 110.

———. "Early History of Madison County and, Incidentally of North Alabama." *Alabama Historical Quarterly* 2 (Summer 1930): 166.

Welsh, Mary. "Reminisces of Old St. Stephens, of More than Sixty-Five Years Ago." *Transactions of the Alabama Historical Society* 3 (1898–99): 221.

Legal References

Acts of the General Assembly of the State of Alabama, 1819. Huntsville, 1820.

Acts Passed at the First Session of the First General Assembly of the Alabama Territory in the Forty-Second Year of American Independence. St. Stephens, AL: Thomas Eastin, Publisher, 1818.

"An Act to Enable the People of Alabama Territory to Form a Constitution and State Government, for the Admission of Such State into the Union, on an Equal Footing with the Original States." Secs. 1 and 5. 15th Congress, 2nd session.

Alabama Constitution of 1819.

Carter, Clarence E., ed. "An Act Establishing the Alabama Territory, March 3, 1817." *Territorial Papers of the United States.* Vol. 18. Washington, D.C.: Government Printing Office, 1937, 53–57.

———. "An Act Providing for the Disposal of Land South of Tennessee, March 3, 1803." *Territorial Papers of the United States.* Vol. 5. Washington, D.C.: Government Printing Office, 1937, 192–205.

Journal of the House of Representatives of the General Assembly of the State of Alabama. Cahawba, AL: Press Office, 1820.

Journal of the House of Representatives of the General Assembly of the State of Alabama. Cahawba, AL: Allen & Drichell, 1821.

Journal of the House of Representatives of the State of Alabama Being the Seventh Annual Session of Said State. Cahawba, AL: William B. Allen, 1826.

Journal of the Legislative Council of the Alabama Territory at the First Session of the General Assembly in the Forty-Third Year of American Independence. St. Stephens, AL: Thomas Eaton. 1818.

Journal of the Senate at the Called Session of the General Assembly of the State of Alabama. Cahawba, AL: Allen & Brickell, 1821.

Journal of the Senate at the Second Session of the General Assembly of the State of Alabama. Cahawba, AL: Allen & Drichell, 1821.

Journal of the Senate of the State of Alabama Being the Eighth Annual Session of the General Assembly of Said State. Tuscaloosa, AL: Grantland and Robinson, 1827.

Journal of the Senate of the State of Alabama Being the Fifth Annual Session of the General Assembly of Said State Cahawba, AL: William B. Allen & Co., 1824.

Journal of the Senate of the State of Alabama Being the Seventh Annual Session of the General Assembly of Said State. Cahawba, AL: William B. Allen, 1826.

Official Journal of the Constitutional Convention of 1819.

"Proclamation," December 30, 1816. In *Indian Affairs: Laws and Treaties.* Vol. II, *Treaties.* Compiled and edited by Charles J. Kappler. Washington, D.C.: Government Printing Office, 1904.

"Resolution Declaring the Admission of the State of Alabama into the Union." 16th Congress, 1st session.

Senate Journal, Alabama Territorial Legislature. February 3, 1818.

Toulmin's Digest of the Laws of the State of Alabama. Cahawba, AL: Ginn & Curtis, 1823.

Toulmin's Mississippi Territory Statutes. N.p., 1807.

Treaty of Cusseta. 1832.

Treaty of St. Stephens. October 24, 1816. 7 Stat. 152.

Treaty with the Cherokee. January 7, 1806. 7 Stat. 101.

Treaty with the Chickasaw. July 23, 1805. 7 Stat. 89.

Turner's Digest of the Laws of the Mississippi Territory. N.p., 1816.

Archival Material

Chambers to Governor W.C.C. Claiborne. RG 2 (Territorial Governor's Papers). Vol. 22, no. 175. Mississippi Department of Archives and History, Jackson, MS.

"Crawley Deposition." In *Correspondence of Andrew Jackson*, edited by John Spenser Bassett (Washington, D.C.: Carnegie Institution, 1926–1935), 1:225–26 n.1.

Ephraim Kirby to William Simpson, March 25, 1804. Ephraim Kirby Manuscripts Collection (1775–1804). Duke University Library, Durham, NC.

"Historical Account: When Tuscaloosa Was the State Capital." James August Anderson Papers MSS.0078, 169a–170a. University Libraries Division of Special Collections, University of Alabama, Tuscaloosa, AL.

J.S.W. Parkin to Jno. R. Parker, May 15, 1819. J.S.W. Parkin Letters, SPR 101. Alabama Department of Archives and History (ADAH), Montgomery, AL.

Matte, Jacqueline A., Doris Brown and Barbara Waddell, comps. *Old St. Stephens: Historical Records Survey*. Rev. ed. St. Stephens Historical Commission, 1999.

William Ely to Clarissa Ely, April 20, 1820; and William Ely to Clarissa Ely, June 2, 1821. William Ely Letters. W.S. Hoole Special Collections Library, University of Alabama, Tuscaloosa, AL.

Newspapers and Magazines

Alabama Republican [Huntsville], September 30, 1817.

Alabama State Intelligencer [Tuscaloosa], January 19, 1831.

Alabama Watchman [Cahawba], August 18, 1820; August 25, 1820; September 29, 1820; December 30, 1820.

Cahawba Gazette, January 7, 1826.

Clinton, Matthew W. "De Soto First in a Long Line of Visitors." *Tuscaloosa News*, April 20, 1969.

Clinton, Thomas P. "The Steamboat Cotton Plant and the Salt Works in Civil War Times." *Tuscaloosa News*, October 18, 1926.

Halcyon and Tombeckbe Public Advertiser [St. Stephens], December 25, 1819; July 6, 1822.

Kershaw, Sarah. "Amid the Ghosts of Alabama." *New York Times*, April 18, 2008.

Niles Weekly Register, February 28, 1818.

Internet References

"Alabama Constitution Village." http://www.earlyworks.com/alabama-constitution-village (accessed January 7, 2014).

"Alabama's Supreme Court Justices, Reuben Saffold." http://www.archives.alabama.gov/judicial/saffold.html (accessed June 27, 2014).

Ambrose, Stephen. "Remembering the Sultana." NationalGeographic.com. http://news.nationalgeographic.com/news/2001/05/0501_river5.html (accessed March 16, 2013).

"Autobiography of Gideon Lincecum." http://nationalhumanitiescenter.org/pds/livingrev/expansion/text2/lincecum.pdf (accessed March 31, 2014).

"The Cahaba Foundation." http://www.cahabafoundation.org/cahawba.html (accessed March 18, 2014).

Dunn, Robert Andrew. "Stand in the School Door." *Encyclopedia of Alabama.* http://www.encyclopediaofalabama.org/face/Article.jsp?id=h-1872 (accessed on April 30, 2014).

"Francis Strother Lyon." http://bioguide.congress.gov/scripts/biodisplay.pl?index=L000542 (accessed November 20, 2013).

"Green Bottom Inn." Huntsville Madison County Public Library Digital Archive. http://digitalarchives.hmcpl.org/cdm/singleitem/collection/p15431coll1/id/63/rec/1 (accessed June 28, 2014).

"Helion Lodge: Birthplace of Masonry in Alabama." http://www.helionlodge.org (accessed December 30, 2013).

"History of Old St. Stephens." http://oldststephens.com/history_of_old_st_stephens.htm (accessed June 22, 2010).

"James Madison from Edwin Lewis." November 21, 1810 (Abstract). Founders Online, National Archives. http:/founders.archives.gov/documents/Madison/03-03-02-0026, ver. 2013-09-28.

Katz, James P. "Autherine Lucy." *Encyclopedia of Alabama.* http://www.encyclopediaofalabama.org/face/Article.jsp?id=h-2489 (accessed April 30, 2014).

Lewis, Herbert J. "Henry Hitchcock." *Encyclopedia of Alabama.* http://www.encyclopediaofalabama.org/face/Article.jsp?id=h-1095 (accessed November, 20, 2013).

———. "Old St. Stephens." *Encyclopedia of Alabama.* http://www.encyclopediaofalabama.org/face/Article.jsp?id=h-1674 (accessed October 21, 2013).

———. "Tuscaloosa." *Encyclopedia of Alabama.* http://www.encyclopediaofalabama.org/face/Article.jsp?id=h-1654 (accessed April 7, 2014).

Mast, Brian. "Fort Tombeckbe." http://www.encyclopediaofalabama.org/face/Article.jsp?id=h-3080 (accessed October 21, 2013).

"The Official Home for the University of Alabama Athletics: Crimson Tide." http://www.rolltide.com/trads/national-championships.html (accessed April 30, 2014).

"Project Digs into Mysteries of the State's First Capital." *Montgomery Advertiser.* http://www.montgomeryadvertiser.com/story/news/local/alabama/2014/06/24/project-digs-mysteries-states-first-capital/11299273 (accessed on June 30, 2014).

Robertson, Ben P. "Lewis Sewell." *Encyclopedia of Alabama.* http://www.encyclopediaofalabama.org/face/Article.jsp?id=h-3004 (accessed June 27, 2014).

Robinson, Mark. "Newtown: The Story of Tuscaloosa's Bygone Rival." Cool Hoole. http://apps.lib.ua.edu/blogs/coolathoole/2013/11/04/newtown-the-story-of-tuscaloosas-bygone-rival/ (accessed April 2, 2014).

Rohr, Nancy M. "The Early Years: Comings and Goings about Town." http://huntsvillehistorycollection.org/hh/index.php?title=The_Early_Years:_Comings_and_Goings_about_Town (accessed January 12, 2014).

Schmidt, Greg. "Huntsville." *Encyclopedia of Alabama.* http://www.encyclopediaofalabama.org/face/Article.jsp?id=h-2498 (accessed January 24, 2014).

Sledge, John. "St. Stephens Historical Overview." American Center for Artists. http://www.americanartists.org/art/article_st_stephens_historical_overview.htm (accessed June 22, 2010).

"The University Club." http://www.universityclub.ua.edu (accessed April 4, 2014).

"The University of Alabama: Did You Know." http://www.ua.edu/quickfacts/know.html (accessed April 30, 2014).

"Volunteers Unearth Alabama's Past at Old St. Stephens." www.alabamasfrontpoarches.org/2010/05/old_st-stephens (accessed November 19, 2013).

Weerts, Christine. "Dinner Meeting Followed Battle." *Selma Times-Journal*, April 24, 2010. http://www.selmatimesjournal.com/2010/04/24/dinner-meeting-followed-battle (accessed March 14, 2414).

"William Crawford, 1784–1849." http://www.almd.uscourts.gov/outreach/docs/CRAWFORD.pdf (accessed November 20, 2013).

Index

T

About the Author

Herbert James "Jim" Lewis earned his BA in history and his law degree from the University of Alabama. He clerked for Associate Justice Robert B. Harwood of the Supreme Court of Alabama, served in the U.S. Air Force in the Judge Advocate General's Office and practiced for twenty-six years as an assistant U.S. attorney in Birmingham, Alabama. In April 2006, the *Alabama Review* published his article concerning one of Alabama's earliest attorneys, and Jim has contributed or edited numerous articles to the comprehensive *Encyclopedia of Alabama.* In March 2013, Jim's first book, *Clearing the Thickets: A History of Antebellum Alabama*, was published by Quid Pro Books of New Orleans, Louisiana.

Visit us at
www.historypress.net

This title is also available as an e-book